What pe

The Magical Sexual Practi.... Egypt

A powerful exploration of the spiritual aspects of sex magic of the ancient Egyptians for the modern occultist and spiritual aspirant alike.

In this fascinating book Judy Hall reminds us of two things, the first is that she is herself an occult scholar of great spiritual insight and knowledge – as well as being the international go-to expert for all things crystal in our modern world. A genius whose academic and mechanical understanding of the magical universe, combined with her intuitive and psychical connection to the deep currents, enables her to create a work that rivals the great arcane peers of our time. Secondly that sex is and always has been something sacred, something truly magical which can be employed physically and spiritually to great ends – the greatest in fact – the alchemical transmutation of the Spirit! A captivating read for the occultist – whether learned or neophyte – as well as anyone drawn to the Egyptian mysteries or those aspiring towards spiritual mastery and ascension. Judy Hall delivers a complex topic in an accessible way for the serious student of magic and the occult.

Edwin Courtenay, author of *The Ascended Masters' Book of Ritual and Prayer* and *Reflections: The Masters Remember* and *The Archangelic Book of Ritual and Prayer*

The ancient Egyptians understood the creative power of sex magic and used it to manifest in the material world, as well as to connect with the divine forces of the universe. Drawing upon the ideas expressed in an early Egyptian papyrus and those of the nineteenth-century occultist and medical doctor, Paschal Beverly Randolph, Judy Hall reveals the secrets of sacred sexual union. Unravelling the mysteries for modern-day seekers is no easy task, but Hall does it with sensitivity and sincerity, while also sharing her own insights. In language both eloquent and accessible, she introduces readers to the magical rites known to initiates for millennia. These practices enable one to harness the tremendous potential of ecstatic sex to gain health, wealth, and happiness. The path doesn't end there, however; it leads beyond the physical realm to union with the Higher Self and All That Is. *The Magical Sexual Practices of Ancient Egypt* is an illuminating, informative, and thoroughly engaging study of the 'mystical marriage', its transformative power, and its value to us in the twenty-first century.

Skye Alexander, author of *Sex Magic for Beginners*

The Magical Sexual Practices of Ancient Egypt

The Alchemy of Night Enchiridion

Also by Judy Hall

Non-Fiction
Crystal Prescriptions
An A-Z guide in 7 volumes

Astro-characters
A writer's guide to creating compelling fictional characters with
the signs of zodiac

Fiction
Torn Clouds
The Alchemy of Night

The Magical Sexual Practices of Ancient Egypt

The Alchemy of Night Enchiridion

Judy Hall

BOOKS

Winchester, UK
Washington, USA

First published by O-Books, 2019
O-Books is an imprint of John Hunt Publishing Ltd., 3 East St., Alresford,
Hampshire SO24 9EE, UK
office1@jhpbooks.net
www.johnhuntpublishing.com
www.o-books.com

For distributor details and how to order please visit the 'Ordering' section on our website.

Text copyright: Judy Hall 2018

ISBN: 978 1 78279 287 1
978 1 78279 288 8 (ebook)
Library of Congress Control Number: 2017964341

A CIP catalogue record for this book is available from the British Library.

Design: Stuart Davies

UK: Printed and bound by CPI Group (UK) Ltd, Croydon, CR0 4YY
US: Printed and bound by Thomson Shore, 7300 West Joy Road, Dexter, MI 48130

We operate a distinctive and ethical publishing philosophy in
all areas of our business, from our global network of authors to
production and worldwide distribution.

Contents

With illustrations by Kristin Wieland
Cover art by Kristin Wieland

Acknowledgements

My deepest thanks to my immensely talented illustrator Kristin Wieland who interpreted my ideas so perfectly.

The Wine Of Love
Oh! when my lady comes, And I with love behold her,
I take her into my beating heart And in my arms enfold her;
My heart is filled with joy divine
For I am hers and she is mine.
Oh! when her soft embraces do give my love completeness,
The perfumes of Arabia anoint me with their sweetness;
And when her lips are pressed to mine
I am made drunk and need not wine.
When we kiss, and her warm lips half open,
I fly cloud-high without beer!
What paradise gained, what fulfilment,
What a heavenly turn of affairs!
– Ancient Egyptian love poem

They who truly love, in their sacred, spiritual passion, strike out this divine spark; partake of that celestial fire; replenish themselves with the quintessence of life itself, grow better, and spiritually strong and beautiful, ripe, morally wealthy, calm, hopeful, attuned to this upper music.
– Paschal Beverly Randolph

Introduction: Sweetening the night

Sex power is God power.
– Dr Paschal B. Randolph, *Eulis*

Sex is the most potent force in the universe. A primal power. A gateway to the divine realm that the ancient Egyptians instinctively recognised. According to an early Egyptian myth, the world came into being through a single-handed act. Creation was self-engendered by the sun god Ra. In other words through masturbation. In the *Book of Knowing* we are told,

> *I had union with my closed hand, and I embraced my shadow as a wife, and I poured seed into my own mouth, and I sent forth from myself issue...*[1]

The story of creation. Nut, the sky goddess, shown in male form, above Geb, the earth god, who is pleasuring himself "pouring his seed into his mouth", alongside a more conventional depiction of Nut and Geb.[2]

Two gods, male and female, were born of this solo-sex act and from there all else followed. The ancient Egyptians were not prudish, they glorified in their bodies and their sexuality. Unafraid to make love to themselves, they also revelled in the uniting of two souls in mutual orgasmic pleasure. The Turin Erotic Papyrus shows a woman seated on a vase, apparently pleasuring herself, while she puts on her make-up – with the assistance of a highly turned-on partner seated on the floor who has his finger in her vagina.³ While an improbable but highly popular Internet legend has it that Cleopatra created a vibrator for herself using a container filled with buzzing bees.⁴

The priests and priestesses of the time utilised the intense energy generated by the sexual act to fuel *heka*, magic. They fertilised, amplified and directed the Power of Sekhem to influence the course of present or future events to their advantage.⁵ They also used it to create mind-blowing orgasms. The term mind-blowing is used advisedly. The resulting cosmic orgasm was more than could be envisaged from the limited perspective of earth.

Recognising that ecstatic sex creates an altered state of bliss consciousness, the natural force was manipulated and shaped by the ancient Egyptians into a magical tool of enormous potency that reached far out into the cosmos and Absolute Oneness – a point beyond separate creation and the multidimensions of consciousness where all becomes one once more. At the same time, the orgasm was embodied, that is, experienced within the physical body. For the ancient Egyptians, contact with the divine was not an abstract, otherworldly concept. It was a fully embodied mystical experience:

> *As a temple ritualist, the Egyptian initiate, in order to be transformed and "see" the deity directly, never leaves his physical body behind in a passive, trance-like state… Fully awake, he enters into a deeper, more profound, mysterious layer of reality and contacts this plane directly, alone and without intermediaries, except for the doubles (Kas) and the souls (Bas). Rituals make his body fully participate in this inner experience.⁶*

The Alchemy of Night process brings about this fully embodied mystical experience, and has unexpected bonuses. The first is the power to create and bring things into manifestation. Something you too can harness, once the process is mastered, to bring additional health, wealth and well-being into your life. You could also utilise the second bonus, activating the Inner Akashic Record, to transform yourself, your ancestral source and the generations to come.

A communication in the night

This book is both a work of non-fiction and of fiction. Not so much channelled as gently infused into my mind. It began with an ancient tome 'dictated' to me as I dreamt a novel, *The Alchemy of Night*. This ancient tome, *The Alchemy of Night Enchiridion*, was communicated to me by Dr Paschal Beverly Randolph, an enigmatic figure. I acted as a literary assistant, an amanuensis. According to Randolph, the tome was an ancient one he had found when travelling in Egypt. In the novel, he copied it and left the original in a hotel safe from where it was rescued and brought to England by Sir H. Rider Haggard. The copy was taken back to America where it formed the basis for Randolph's system of sex magic.

An African-American medical doctor, Randolph was an occultist, Spiritualist, trance medium, abolitionist and prolific writer whose specialty was sex in all its guises. Founder of the Brotherhood of Eulis and, as I later discovered during my follow-up research, author of *Magia Sexualis: Sexual Practices for Magical Power* and other books on sexual magic. The similarities between that book and the tome are striking. To the extent that I came to believe that Randolph was actually speaking to me from the Other World.

However, although Randolph's translation of the Pharaoh's ancient text is the talismanic core of *The Alchemy of Night*, the language of the tome is turgid, convoluted and impenetrable. I quickly dropped my intention of including it within the novel in its entirety. But I was urged by my communicator to bring it into the light once more. To translate The Alchemy of Night

3

into a process of sexual initiation and Power of Sekhem-raising that could be utilised by the modern world. To work with and interpret the practice so that it would be accessible to all. This book is the result.

Each chapter of the arcane tome is given as originally dictated. It includes interpretations by Randolph (P.R.B.), but whose words are equally outdated and somewhat obscure, together with addendum notes added by E.A.W.B.[7] There then follows a contemporary explanation, more suited to the modern practitioner. As will be seen, it is essential to read all three versions as this activates a metaphysical paradigm within the brain and subtle energy system.

In the novel, the tome is a book-within-a-book. The spark that enflames my protagonist, taking her from an innocent young woman into full womanhood. But it quickly flowered into something more: a process for mastering the psycho-spiritual sexual energy known as 'the Power of Sekhem'. It brings about a mystic marriage at the inner and outer levels, culminating in sacred union and a cosmic orgasm. The technique is known as the Alchemy of Night.

Randolph, a fascinating character full of contradictions and paradoxes, is the protagonist in the third volume of *The Alchemy of Night* trilogy. The first volume, in which Randolph appears as a central and yet largely unseen peripheral character, tells the tale of the shade of an ancient Egyptian Pharaoh who failed to move into the next world and who wreaks havoc in the present time. Such a character is fully supported by Randolph:

Not all invisible onlookers, however, are to be counted in along with seraphs and angels... People may laugh as much as they please at the idea of wicked, mean, obsessing, tantalizing, tempting beings, or at the old notions of the alchemists and others of that ilk; my researches and experience tell a far different story. When it is asserted that there is no mysterious means whereby ends both good

and ill can be wrought at any distance; that the so-called "spells,"
"charms" and "projects" are mere notions, having no firmer
foundation than superstition or empty air alone; – then I flatly
deny all such assertions, and affirm that the conclusions arrived
at are so reached by persons wholly ignorant of the invisible world
about us, and of the inner powers of the human mind.
– Dr P.B. Randolph, *Seership!*

(Such visitations can be guarded against by those in the know,
see 'A note about the dark side' in Chapter 1.)

The mystic marriage

The intention of the alchemical process is to bring about a mystical
marriage. A mystic marriage is a balancing of apparent dualities
and a return to integrated multidimensional consciousness or
'Absolute Oneness' as the ancient tome puts it. However, the
mystic marriage is also a process that leads to harnessing the
magic of creation. Something at which the Egyptians excelled.
Until now, that *heka*, or manifestation magic, was a closely
guarded, esoteric temple secret available only to those carefully
initiated into its practices during long years of training.

Mystic marriage

One of the strongest soul bonds of all was created in the
ancient temples and in occult and esoteric orders between
two soulmates or twinflames. The mystic marriage was
intended to last 'for eternity'. A different, positive and
present-life growth-enhancing form of the mystical
marriage is the marriage of our own inner male and female
energies integrated with the divine spark within us all.

How do we know that the mystic marriage occurred in ancient

Egypt? Well, the author and metaphysician Murry Hope was handed, by a stranger on a train, an ancient Egyptian papyrus detailing eight of its steps. Unfortunately the final steps were missing. She gave a lecture on it at the College of Psychic Studies in London sometime in the late 1980s/early 90s. To my knowledge, she did not write a book on the subject but I took a liberty with this, and other matters, in the pages of the novel. Artistic licence of which Murry would undoubtedly have approved.

Endings and beginnings

The *Enchiridion*, as dictated, lacked an ending, so the question was raised as to the exact purpose of the Alchemy of Night. In the novel, it is misconceived as being the creation of a physical magical child into which the shade of the ancient Pharaoh could reincarnate. By the end of the novel, the main characters suspect that this may not be the ultimate purpose (something to be pursued further in the third volume of the trilogy). In the first chapter of the tome, it is stated that "mere sensual gratification is not the aim of the Eternal Ones", but the ultimate goal is not explicitly defined. In this present book, the question is resolved through entirely new codas that complete the process of magical sexual initiation and harness the primal sexual force to the magic of creation and healing.

The Power of Sekhem

The Power of Sekhem is raised after the Fires, or Flames, of Mut and Min, the physical sexual force that is known as kundalini in Eastern systems. A higher resonance, the Power of Sekhem is a subtle, but extremely dynamic, psycho-spiritual orgasmic energy that lies coiled at the base of the etheric spine and the sacrum, 'the sacred bone', until aroused.

When the Power of Sekhem reaches the crown chakra, it then activates higher chakras linking to the subtle soul-bodies to open transcendent knowing. The Power irradiates the cells of the physical and subtle bodies with a new, lighter resonance. One that literally en-lightens. It awakens the lightbody and the ability to assimilate higher dimensional frequencies on earth. Expanded beyond the conventional seven chakras, the Power of Sekhem unites the soul-bodies and the highest aspects of one's Self, or a couple, in a sacred marriage. It then opens the way to harness the magic of creation.

Engaging the whole being

True teaching is not an accumulation of knowledge. It is an awakening of consciousness which goes through successive stages.
– Ancient Egyptian saying

It is now time to begin the alchemical working. Sex magic requires setting aside the ego and actually *doing* the practice, immersing yourself in it wholeheartedly, and *being* in harmony with each other when working with a partner. It is nothing less than total participation of mind, body, spirit and soul. Surrendering to, and being swept up in, the process. This is not an intellectual exercise to be undertaken by the mind alone. Body and soul are equally involved. The mind has to be willing and able to transcend everyday – consensual – reality and move into the wider reaches of metaphysical and spiritual awareness.

So, engaging in "the willing suspension of disbelief",[8] join me in experiencing the magical practices of an ancient land to invoke a spiritual and sexual conjugation of the soul and ultimately harness the forces of creation.

Your hand in my hand,
My soul inspired,
My heart in bliss,
Because we go together.
– Chester Beatty Papyrus

Chapter 1

Using this book

This chapter contains essential preliminary information. Please do not skip it as otherwise a vital part of the alchemical process may be disregarded, resulting in difficulties later in the process.

As above, so below.

The ancient Egyptians believed that 'as above, so below. As within, so without'. There was a causal relationship between acts in the physical world and those in the spiritual. This means that the rites in this book operate at two levels: the physical that incorporates the senses and bodily sensations; and the metaphysical that includes thoughts, imagination, spiritual beliefs, multidimensional consciousness and opening to the divine. The more you immerse yourself in this all-encompassing worldview, the greater will be your success with *The Alchemy of Night*. You must be open to erotic arousal at every level of your being, and able to stimulate that same level of intimate response in your partner, if you have one.

Structure and repetition

In this *Enchiridion*, the pages of the ancient tome are interleaved with modern commentaries. Even though it may appear to be repetitious, do read them all in order. Perusing each of them in turn drops the ancient Pharaoh's concepts deeper and deeper into your mind, even though they may appear obscure at first. The human brain processes information through the establishment of patterns. Three is the smallest number of elements – or repetitions – required to create a pattern. Information is, therefore, given three times, and each stage is practised a minimum of three times. P.B.R.'s commentary provides a level of understanding of the concepts, although couched in the language of his time, supplemented by explanatory notes from E.A.W.B. Moving on to the modern commentary and working through the associated rite brings enlightenment *and the information is retained more readily for having first established a metaphysical pattern.*

So, repetition is key. Although it is tempting to read ahead and work with the rites that appeal most, the greatest benefit is obtained from *The Alchemy of Night* process by following the steps slowly in the order in which they appear. Take the time to become intimately familiar with each one. Practise each rite at least three times. They are carefully crafted to prepare you for ultimate soul union and transcension of the small self to integrate with the sacred, divine, Self. The series of initiations can be worked alone or with a soul-partner (see Soulmate or Twinflame? in Chapter 4).

If co-working with a partner, do not move on to the next stage until you have each fully mastered a rite. This was the way it was worked in ancient Egypt. It bonded the two souls together in a mystic marriage that, ultimately, became sacred union. However, if you are working alone, it is possible to complete the initiations to integrate your own masculine and feminine energies, moving from duality to wholeness and integration with your divine Highest Self. Simply follow the stages that are appropriate to the gender-body you currently occupy and use the power of your imagination to complete the steps that require an opposite gender-body.

If you do not currently have a physical partner, work up to the stage of making the inner mystic marriage and move on to ultimate union with the divine, harnessing the power of creation. Then repeat the stages, keeping pace with an appropriate partner should you meet one. If you are working with a partner of the same gender, it is perfectly possible to complete a mystic marriage between you.

The inner mystic marriage

The inner mystic marriage unites the various parts of one's soul and Highest Self that have been male and female in other lives, or integrates the anima and animus carried through those lives. It can be seen as bringing together the two halves of the soul that Plato says were split so long ago (see page 52). It unites inner masculine and feminine qualities, bringing us into inner wholeness. Making this mystical marriage is a profound step forward in spiritual evolution. It means we no longer have to look 'out there' for the perfect partner to complete us. We find, and integrate, all the qualities within our own Self.

As a step along the way, we may meet a seemingly perfect partner 'out there' – a soulmate – who mirrors to us an unseen and unrecognised part of our soul. But, at some stage, we need to recognise and own the qualities of that part in our inner self. This is the moment when our 'soulmate' must withdraw to allow us to integrate those qualities. If we have already found a twinflame (see pages 52–55), our twinflame must stand aside long enough for personal inner union to take place – although it is much more usual to meet a twinflame after the inner integration is complete. You can invite a twinflame into your life (see Appendix III) at any stage. Once the inner marriage is made, we go into relationship not as a lopsided half-person looking for someone to make us whole – seeking our 'other half' – but as a whole person who has something unique to offer in relationship: the whole-self of our true being.[9]

> *There was the Door to which I found no key,*
> *There was the Veil through which I might not see.*
> *Some little talk awhile of Me and Thee*
> *There was – and then no more of Thee and Me.*
> – The Rubaiyat of Omar Khayyam

Intention, aspiration and imagination

As you work through this book, bear in mind that three things make magical working go smoothly.

- **Focused intention.** The higher will, rather than the personal ego, is specifically directed towards a precise objective.
- **Finely-tuned aspiration.** An energised mind reaches for fulfilment of the highest possible outcome for that intention.
- **Honed imagination.** Fired up, magical imagination brings the process to life on the inner planes and then manifests it on the outer. With a powerful imagination, everything is possible.

Keeping a magical journal

When working through a magical alchemical process, keep a journal in which you record your experiences, your aspirations and intentions, and your successes. The purpose of the journal is not only to record your progress but also to identify and attune to your own internal sexual rhythms. Begin by noting the time of day and the moon-phase, track your menstrual cycle if you have one, and your mood at the time. Also any distractions or stresses occurring. You will quickly pick out the most propitious time for the work, which may or may not accord with the timing the ancient Prince identified.

Writing with a pen and paper clarifies insights and brings moments of en-lighten-ment, accessing details you didn't consciously know had occurred. You'll find yourself having 'aha' moments when you say to yourself, "I don't remember experiencing that, but…" – which may sound strange but you'll soon discover what this means if you write spontaneously. Include all that you recall from the rites *no matter how insignificant details may seem at the time.* The pieces will integrate in time.

11

Bear in mind that *The Alchemy of Night* is an ongoing, holistic process that occurs at multilevels of your being. It could take a while to filter down to the physical level, 'below', from higher consciousness, 'above' – and vice versa. The alchemy does not simply take place while you are 'working the rites'. Your journal will help you to look back over a transformational jigsaw that may only make sense with the benefit of hindsight.

The Ultradian rest cycle

Although the ancient Prince identified the periods around sunrise and sunset as being when an initiate is most sexually responsive, there is another cycle of which you could take advantage. You are at your most receptive and intuitively, rather than intellectually, aware during the rest phase of the ultradian cycle. The ultradian cycle has a profound effect on which hemisphere of your brain is active during a one and a half to two-hour period that cycles throughout the twenty-four-hour circadian rhythm. In the comparatively brief ultradian cycle, high activity is followed by a twenty minute 'low' or resting period in which your parasympathetic nervous system is activated and your intuitive right brain is switched on. Your neurophysiological system realigns itself and you are more likely to be able to relax and slip into an altered state of awareness – or to integrate the changes brought about by the alchemical process. It is particularly helpful for the rites that require active imagination on your part. Attuning to your personal cycle vastly improves your ability to disconnect from the external world and simply *allow*. It is the ideal time to practise the rites in this book as it assists the embodiment of the Power of Sekhem.[10]

Identifying the rest phase

This rest-phase period is characterised by:

- The outside world 'disappearing'

- The internal world becoming more vivid
- Difficulty in concentrating
- Exceedingly short attention span
- Mental fuzziness
- Low energy and fatigue
- Daydreams and sleepiness
- An urge to take a break from what you are doing
- Desperate desire for a cup of coffee, chocolate or a cigarette
- Yawning and sighing
- Irritability, discomfort and fleeting depression
- Prickling or unfocused eyes, buzzing ears
- An inability to hear or understand what is said to you the first time around
- Increased use of your hands if you find it difficult to explain something
- Increased visual imagery if you are writing or talking.

Take advantage of this natural rhythm by creating time out from your daily activities. Remove yourself from all external distractions. Breathe deeply and slowly, let yourself fall into a reverie (similar to the hypnagogic state you experience as you fall asleep or awaken). Don't try to focus, ask questions or concentrate. Simply be with what is. However, the ultradian rest phase is also an extremely potent time to practise the stage of sexual alchemy that you have reached, or to set your intention.

The 'Beloveds'

In the ancient tome, the Prince and P.B.R. speak of 'the beloveds', above and below. The 'beloved below' is the physical magical partner with whom you are being bonded step-by-step in mystic marriage (although having a physical partner is not essential for *The Alchemy of Night* process). The 'beloved above' is your own divine Highest Self to whom you are being bonded in sacred marriage. Ultimately your whole soul is unified by the upward flow of the Power of Sekhem joining with the transcendent light of 'above' and then being embodied 'below'.

Choosing a partner for magical sexual working

As the bonding in *The Alchemy of Night* is intended to be lifelong – if not for eternity as was the original temple intention – selection of an empathetic, totally harmonious, physical 'beloved' is crucial. A couple need to share common ideals, a matching sex drive and aligned spiritual intention. A mutual view of the body as sacred and the erotic as divine is essential. Profoundly honest communication and a deep level of trust are required at all levels between the partners. As this process requires total surrender of the ego and the personal will, a partner who is self-centred and arrogant is unlikely to be able to surrender to union with the divine and will not be able to enter into sacred marriage.

Randolph suggests that "no wicked person could truly love and remain wicked." Nevertheless, it is a brave soul indeed who would willingly enter into partnership in such an undertaking. The "wicked person" would have to be utterly wedded to the intention to transform Self and soul at all levels. It is one of the great lessons of soulwork that this cannot be forced upon someone, or undertaken on behalf of another. In other words, no one can do it for you. Great love may overcome obstacles, but it requires a dedication beyond the capacity of most people. With the ability to remain resolutely dispassionate and detached from results, simply holding a space in which the transformation could occur *if the other person is doing their own work*. So never, under any circumstances, enter into *The Alchemy of Night* process with the intention of it transforming or reforming your partner, only yourself. You, and you alone, are responsible for the health and well-being of your own soul. You are not required to become a saviour, rescuer, victim or martyr to 'love'. Such a soul drama has no place in metaphysical or magical working of any kind.

This process is not a recipe for fixing a less-than-ideal

partnership. Alchemy cannot transform a bad relationship into a great one. Although it will transform a relationship that is already good into the best it could be.

Fidelity, both physical and psychological, is required. This is not a process that can be switched on and off at will. Nor can a new partner be substituted partway through. A vital component of the process is working together in tandem, at the same pace, to activate the chakras, physical and spiritual bodies *simultaneously* with each other.

Nevertheless, the practice may, to a great extent, be worked alone up to and including 'marriage with the eternal one'. This brings about union with your divine Highest Self and the greater whole, the godhead 'All That Is'.

If you have a non-magically-compatible sexual partner who is not on the same pathway, a period of sexual abstinence may be required whilst you complete the process for yourself. Do not attempt to involve such a partner in *The Alchemy of Night* as it would create false bonds that could tie your souls together inappropriately and for far longer than you may have anticipated.

Past life contacts

Meeting someone with whom you have had a past life relationship can be an overwhelming sensation, one that 'sucker punches' you in the base and sacral chakras. The pull can be immense. But it may be inappropriate. It may feel as though this is 'The One'. But don't tumble too quickly into bed – and especially not into *The Alchemy of Night* process. The soul bond needs to be at the highest level and previous life relationships tend to make themselves felt at an extremely physical level that may not reflect the true potential of the soul bond. As I said in *The Soulmate Myth*:

> *You meet. Bells ring, the world turns rosy pink, bluebirds weave their dancing flight, and for a few weeks – or months, perhaps even*

years – everything is sublime, you are with 'The One'. The one person who can make you happy and complete. The person you love without question or restraint. The one you've searched for all your life, were created for. But then it begins, little niggling doubts that you push aside until the next time, or a monstrous great betrayal you cannot ignore. Is this really the one, can your other half really be the source of so much pain, so much soul scouring?

Wonderful, marvellous, the best thing that ever happened, your other half – or the biggest delusion ever? This is the question that lies at the heart of the soulmate dilemma. Many people are still reeling from meeting a soulmate years after the event, others yearn for what might have been... These wondrous beings sweep into our life, lust and desire in their wake, they fire up our lower chakras pushing out all that is outworn and outgrown. They prod and poke, wake us up, drive us from a stultifying relationship or into living out our soul's purpose – or not as the case so often is if the initial attraction is misunderstood. Sometimes, they offer us love ever after, but equally often they flow out of our lives again when their task is complete.[11]

So, check carefully before assuming that, just because all your chakras light up at that first meeting, you actually have met the perfect partner with whom to undertake *The Alchemy of Night*. That wave of lust may simply be a way of energetically saying, "Hi, nice to see you again." It does not necessarily mean "and here we go again." You may need to acknowledge the contact – and then run like hell. Or take the time to discover why you've come into contact again. Previous twinflame relationships tend to be felt in the heart as an all-encompassing cloud of unconditional love enveloping your whole being. This is the one to move towards and gently explore the possibilities!

The difference between a soulmate and contact based on a past life relationship that may be past-its-sell-by-date, and one with a twinflame with whom a mystic marriage has been made in the past *and is still relevant today* is explored further in 'Soulmate or twinflame' on page 52. If a relationship is past-its-sell-by-date, tie cutting between you is essential before you move on, as is outdated contract dissolution. (See Appendix IV.)

Tie cutting and contract dissolution

Tie cutting is a helpful preliminary to *The Alchemy of Night* process. Tie cutting does not cut off any unconditional love that there may be between you and your partner. But it does cut off all the oughts, shoulds, if-onlys, buts, karma, old soul contracts and unrealised expectations carried forward from other lives, or indeed the present one. Renegotiating any soul contracts between you is also essential. It leaves you energetically clear, de-cluttered, deprogrammed and ready to input the higher vibration that is *The Alchemy of Night*. (See Appendix IV.)

The magical child

In the novel *The Alchemy of Night*, the ancient prince is, apparently, endeavouring to use the process to create from his own essence a physical 'magical child' into which his soul can be reborn. This is a misunderstanding of the intent behind the process – although a child born through such a union will have a rather special nature. The child, naturally and intuitively, will be more in touch with the highest spiritual aspects of the self than is usual in children born of a non-sacred sexual act.

A magical child born of alchemy lives on the subtle planes of existence beyond the physical. This is a child of soul and spirit that can become a guide, mentor and inspirational daemon – a benevolent, supranatural being with a nature between the divine and the human. The magical child may also be a 'seed of intention' that grows in the creative matrix of the cosmic womb. Such a 'child' is in touch with the highest aspirations of the overall soul of its creator, or creators, and acts as a guardian for the purest manifestation of soul purpose.

It is hardly surprising that the word 'daemon' has been adopted in computer language to mean a program that runs as an unobtrusive background process that is activated by a specific event or condition, rather than being under the direct control of an interactive user. 'The ghost in the machine' could perhaps be said to be 'the daemon in the soul-body.' The magical child becomes a force that impels towards soul evolution and self-transcension, and which harnesses the power of creation and manifestation. (*See Codas Two and Three.*)

A note on abstinence

A short period of abstinence, 'celibacy', together with psychological faithfulness to 'the beloveds above and below' may be called for during the preparatory stages of the alchemical process. The Prince warns that "desire must be controlled until the appointed time." An edict common to much magical working. But it does not mean the abandonment of desire, or indeed of orgasm. It simply means abstaining from sexual congress with someone other than yourself during the initial stages, and then working in tandem with a compatible magical-physical partner according to the rhythm of the Alchemy of Night process.

Fidelity to the process is what is called for. It is the *mastering* of the orgasmic force that is so vital. Keep in mind that the final aim is mastery, not abstinence. A man must learn the art of orgasm without ejaculation so that the physical sexual force (kundalini) is pushed upwards a higher vibration to become the Power of Sekhem. This is so that the energies, physical and metaphysical, can be attuned, focused and prepared for integration, equilibrium and transcension to a higher plane. Mastery includes moving the Power of Sekhem through the chakras and the subtle bodies, the Highest Self, the soul, the cosmos and, ultimately, the divine. When full sexual union on all levels does occur, it is all the more potent and powerful for having waited. Literally mind-blowing. And the force can then be harnessed to magically bring about a desired outcome or to control one's destiny, a true Alchemy of Night.

A note about the dark side

Ra controlling the forces of darkness.

Ancient Egyptian thought envisaged a duality woven into the matrix fabric of the created universe. Complementary forces: positive and negative, yin and yang, masculine and feminine, light and dark. In Egyptian mythology, one force constantly battled to bring light, literally enlightenment, and the opposite force to create chaos and 'endarkenment'. This was epitomised by the myths of the brother-gods Osiris and Set and their ongoing battle for control. Osiris symbolised the fertile Nile Valley, Set the arid desert beyond. Similarly, the sun god Ra battled the serpent Apophis each night to overcome the forces of darkness and chaos – and so be reborn in the morning. But it was a delicate tipping point, a balance that could go either way. Temple rituals ensured that equilibrium was maintained.

In *The Alchemy of Night Enchiridion*, the ancient Pharaoh is at pains to stress that the process and rites must be carried out with due ceremony and respect. With 'right-mindedness' – and in the correct order. "No step can be circumvented, nothing can move out of its appointed place." It is this carefully constructed order, reflecting the manifested order within the universe, which protects an initiate whilst on the path. Step off that path, and chaos may intervene. This means that, provided you keep your feet firmly on the path – and your will focused on your goal of sacred, spiritual marriage and magical creation – no harm will befall you.

If you do falter and encounter the dark side, as do the protagonists in *The Alchemy of Night* novel, steps have to be taken to counteract it – and to protect yourself while doing so. In the novel, this is achieved by use of a twentieth century magician's take on an ancient pentagram ritual. It is utilised to banish unfriendly spirits, or for protection.[12] It also sets up sacred space in which to carry out your spiritual and magical work. All it takes is focused will and intention, and a sharply honed imagination. Tools that every sexual magician requires for successful working.

Creating safe space

- On the floor, draw a five-pointed star with chalk or your finger, or imagine it. You could outline it with a crystal wand. Start at the top and trace it in front of you. It will burst into fiery flames. Return to the first point to close the star.

- Stand in the centre facing east. Breathe slowly and regularly, fully releasing the breath before you inhale again, with a long pause between the breaths.
- Raise your hands to your forehead with your hands together as though praying. See light streaming down to form a ball above your head. Intone the word *Light* as you do so.
- Bring your hands to your heart. Draw a fiery pentagram in front of your chest.
- With your hands over your heart, turn south and draw another pentagram.
- With your hands over your heart, turn to the west and draw another pentagram.
- With your hands over your heart, turn north and draw another pentagram.
- Say: "I call on the gods to protect me, filling the space around me with Light. For about me are the flames of the pentagram."
- See the light above your head coming in a beam of light straight down through your body towards the centre of the Earth anchoring you. This is your protection.

Alternatively, you can trace the pentagrams in the air or in your lap, facing the four directions as you do so where possible but this is not essential.

When moving through the stages in this book, draw a pentagram around your bed or the space in which you are working to create safe, sacred space.

Visualisation

Visualisation is one of the most potent tools used in the Alchemy of Night. It uses the inner eye to bring a setting or a partner into being. Looking up to the space above and between your eyebrows, whilst keeping your eyes closed, helps images to form. But some people will never 'see' anything because they are kinaesthetic (feeling orientated) rather than visual. If you are one of those people, simply trust that the setting is there. Concentrate on the sensual side, *feel* it in your body, sense it, smell it, believe it.

The preparation and relaxation below will assist most of the rites within this book.

Preparation for visualisation:

- Sit in a chair with your feet on the floor and your hands resting gently on your knees. When you are comfortably settled, close your eyes. Take ten slow, deep breaths. As you breathe out, let go of any tension you may be feeling. As you breathe in, draw in a sense of peace and relaxation. Consciously let go of your everyday worries and concerns and allow yourself to be at peace. Bring your awareness deep into yourself and let any thoughts simply float on by.
- Breathe gently, establishing an even rhythm. Allow your eyelids to grow heavy and lie softly. Then let waves of relaxation flow through your body with each breath. Take it from the top of your head, to your fingertips and down to your toes.
- Without opening your eyes, look up to the point

immediately above and between your eyebrows and let your inner eye open.

- Continue with the rite as appropriate.

Closing down

Closing down after a rite is equally as important as opening up correctly in safe space, as otherwise you may leave yourself open to subtle invasion or energy leaching. So complete each rite with the following close down.

Closing down

- When you are ready to close, withdraw from your connections with your magical partner, or with the Highest Self or the divine. Thank them for their assistance.
- Surround yourself with a protective bubble of light that goes all around you and under your feet. Crystallise the outer edges of your aura (the biomagnetic field that surrounds you) with your mind or hold an actual crystal.
- Then slowly return your awareness to the room and open your eyes.
- Feel your feet on the floor and your connection to the earth with a grounding cord going deep into the earth holding you firmly in incarnation.
- Get up and do something practical, or have a hot drink to ground you.

Protection and close-down crystals: Apache Tear, Black Tourmaline, Flint, Hematite, Mohawkite, Shungite, Smoky Quartz.

The Alchemy of Night Enchiridion

A Treatise on Sexual Thaumaturgy
And the Practice thereof
The Prince Khem Yar Khepher'set,
Supreme Ruler of Khemit and the Two Lands
Being a true and accurate account of the Finding and
Transcription of an authentic papyrus from Ancient Egypt
With

A Commentary on the Practices therein
Dr Paschal B. Randolph

Ohio 1862
Foreword and Addendum notes provided by E.A.W.B.
Keeper of Egyptian Antiquities, British Museum, London
Reprinted for private circulation 1921

Chapter 2

A Lost Key

The foreword and introduction to the ancient tome require little interpretation other than an explanation of the various soul-bodies. In ancient Egypt the soul was multilayered. This is a fairly straightforward account of the finding and return of a lost arcane Egyptian manuscript to the modern world, authenticated by an Egyptian specialist.

The Alchemy of Night Enchiridion

Foreword

A Lost Key

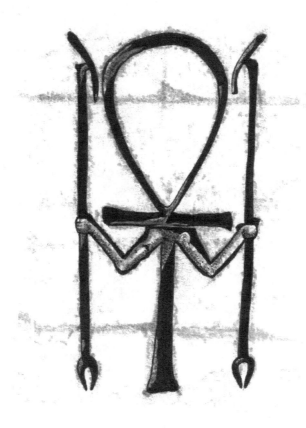

The Alchemy of Night Enchiridion

The forgotten key

It is with great pleasure that I write this introduction to the new printing for private circulation of an ancient classic text first made available in the latter part of the 19th century by the Southern American Gentleman Esotericist Dr Paschal Beverly Randolph, but since lost. Herein lies a forgotten key to spiritual development through Arcane Carnal Lore that provides us with a practical method for developing the Hidden Powers of Man. Here, thaumaturgy, called by the ignorant wonderworking, reveals the secrets of creation. Love, and the nuptive moment, unlocks the doors of the Spirit and discloses the secret of Eternal Life.

I am sincerely grateful that this work was saved for posterity by the distinguished writer and learned Gentleman Egyptologist, Sir H. Rider Haggard of the County of Norfolk. My old friend acquired the typescript and a copy of the original papyrus on one of his expeditions to the town of Luxor in Upper Egypt. It had been left in safekeeping by the author Dr Paschal Beverly Randolph on one of his sojourns there, but he had not returned to claim it. The hotel manager placed it into the hands of my old friend, having learned of Randolph's death. Recognising its potential value and seeking authentication of the translation of the hieroglyphs and the magical system therein, Haggard cautiously handed the package to me one evening on the balcony of our Cairo hotel. An artefact such as this was not to be displayed before the eyes of the uninitiated amateur Egyptologist, such as is found frequenting the hotel lobby in the hope of chancing upon such a prize. And indeed, as one such rudely interrupted our exploration by climbing up from the street below, the manuscript was hastily bundled away before I could examine it. I was not to set eyes on it for several years, the

Great War having intervened in the meantime.

It was, therefore, with some trepidation and not a little excitement that, in my basement room at the British Museum, I examined the tattered, foxed and blotched pages that had suffered from being left out in the sun at some time heretofore. It looked rather as though some modern day Egyptian fellahin had used it for his ablutions before deciding that it might be sold to a touristica. The printed word was, however, intelligible enough and fortunately, the hieroglyphs and interlinked demotic script had, although the ink had faded, been meticulously transcribed alongside and I was able to assert the veracity of the translation and begin to ascertain the source. According to P.B.R., the original papyrus manuscript was incomplete, there were numerous lacunae. Some pages being fragmentary and others altogether lost: nevertheless, it was possible for him to reconstruct many of the initiation rituals contained therein and to ascertain the stages through which an initiate passed to reach Nuptive Adepthood. Union with the Divine and union with the soul of the Beloved. Although, unfortunately, the final pages were entirely missing as were the last stages. What was totally lacking was the objective towards which the work was directed. We do not know what would have materialised from the mystic joining. P.B.R. assumed that it was a rite complete in itself that allowed for prayers to be made manifest. I myself have reservations. I believe that it was intended for a specific purpose, but what that purpose was, we cannot know. We may, however, utilise the steps to the mystic marriage to bring ourselves nearer to the Ultimate. To hone our powers and Be the Best That We May Be.

The original work seemed to me to be from prior to the earliest known dynasty of the Pharaohs. The hieroglyphs were somewhat naïve, the language arcane, and the demotic script had clearly been added for the assistance of later generations of priests. For priestly it indeed was. Instructions such as this were not for the eyes of the laity – and remain so today. It is my opinion that only those adepts with a high degree of initiation into the esoteric mysteries can possibly have mastered the controlled will and high spiritual intentions required to bring about sexual congress with the Divine within the sacred union of ritual matrimony. To have made a union with another human soul would surely create a further entity, a conjoined spirit, but to what end we cannot know.

This instruction manual of sexual thaumaturgy is purportedly the work of an ancient Prince. It is an authoritative guide to a precisely formulated system of beliefs and practices that must have been ancient when he first recorded his magical text. The teachings would have been passed from mouth to mouth unsullied by scribal errors. It is a recension of a seven thousand year history, pre-dynastic shamanism in its purest form. The translation into our modern English is difficult as many passages and allusions remain obscure but I have, I hope, in some small way expanded on our understanding of the obfuscations found in the 1868 translation.

The ancient Prince was at pains to extol his reader towards care of the soul, which in ancient Khem, the modern reader must understand, was not one indivisible unit as in our exalted Christian belief. The *Ka* or etheric double was the portion of the soul that incarnated with an independent existence, the shadowy twin tied to the *Khat* or physical body. The *Ka* acted as a vessel for the *Ba* soulbird, which remained close to the Earth although it could enter the heavens to negotiate with the Gods. The *Ka* held a man's unique identity, his personality and his shadow. After death, the *Ka* was attached to the tomb and could not roam if the appropriate propitiatory rituals were observed. If angered or thwarted, the *Ka* could haunt the living and interfere maliciously with their lives. The *Ba* was the soul that flew free above but which was said to reside in the physical heart. The *Ba* had substance and form and could become corporeal or incorporeal at will. After death, the *Ba* travelled to the celestial realms but could revisit the *Ka* in the tomb. The soul's power, the *Sekhem*, was a personification of a man's vital force which could travel to the celestial realms but which could also be confined in the tomb. The *Akhar* was the divine spark that animated all: the God-within.

The *Khu* was perceived as a luminous, intangible shape, what metaphysicians today describe as the Body of Light, the subtle etheric body that contains the whole and which, to the Egyptian eye, transcends death but which had to be activated and integrated with other soul parts, 'illuminated' in the Egyptian, so that it could function in the hereafter. The *Khu* was the spiritual intelligence of the soul. However, by the use of magical incantations, the *Khu* could be deliberately imprisoned in the tomb with the *Ka* after death and considerable care was taken during the mummification process to avoid this catastrophe except in the most heinous of circumstances. The Alchemy of Night system of thaumaturgy unites the major portions of the soul in persons of both genders to create a truly integrated and immortal whole, the incorruptible *Sakhu*, which can function independently during life and which will, unless constrained, after death, travel in the Body of Light to the celestial realm to be with the Gods.

The rite unites each with their Twin Flame, the complement of their soul. In the rare event that two persons who were joined throughout eternity in this way should return to Earth again, or parts of whose souls have remained close to or upon Earth rather than travelling to the Other World, they will find themselves irresistibly attracted towards each other no matter in what body they are incarnated – be it the physical or one of the soul bodies. One can only speculate on the complications to which this could lead. However, as certain portions of the papyrus, and the end itself, are lost, we cannot know the ultimate goal towards which this rite of thaumaturgy was leading. Clearly there were steps beyond the mystic marriage but these portions are missing, deliberately torn out one might assume. A sad loss indeed for metaphysics, and for the human soul. It is possible that P.B.R., in assuming that the rite of union was the completion as and of itself, may have made a grave error. Nevertheless, his intimations following how he received the papyrus hint at a higher understanding obtained beyond that conveyed in these pages and, perhaps, taught within his highly secretive organisation.

The Prince's precepts are ones that we would do well to follow today, however. He held that marriage and fidelity within that union was the only road that would lead to embodiment of the Divine presence. Thus a priest and priestess should also be man and wife cleaving only unto themselves. An exhortation that modern esoteric groups should duly note. The Prince Khem Yar Khepher'set, Justified, peace be upon his name, recognised love within sacred sexuality and the bonds of mystic marriage as the foundation for the spiritual life. His unshakeable certainty that humanity was created with dual-gender expressly so that we might commingle our natures underlies the whole Work. It is the highest calling to which a soul may aspire. As he so perceptively points out: "The soul needs love as much as the body requires food. Love-starvation, the nostalgia or homesickness of the soul, is the most terrible evil that can oppress the human spirit." As P.B.R. himself taught, no doubt from the same source: "No wicked person can truly love and remain wicked. That is the redemptive salvatory and alchemical power of the divine principle."

E.A.W.B.
Savage Club, London, 1920

Modern commentary

The Egyptian soul

We will be looking in greater depth at concepts such as the twinflame a little later. But, before commencing the rites, as E.A.W.B. points out, it is helpful to have an understanding of the Egyptian view of the soul. This was not a separate, unified body, but rather a series of loosely connected, independent subtle bodies that occupied a space between the worlds rather than being located in purely physical space. Egyptologists – and metaphysicians – do not always agree on the exact translation of the names for the soul-bodies. These are the titles utilised within this book.

The Egyptian soul-bodies

- **The Khat or Kha:** the physical body that could decay after death but which was the vehicle for the soul and consciousness whilst in incarnation. The subtle body Khat carried the generative force of a soul after death.
- **The Ka:** the imperishable 'etheric double' that could either inhabit the body or, after death, the tomb. It was the vital essence, the 'life force' that animated the human being. The Ka carried the personality that developed during incarnation and could lead an independent existence.
- **The Ba:** the immortal and transcendent 'soulbird' that had its home in the heart. The Ba had a powerful personality and strong elemental needs for food and sex. Hence, until reintegrated, it required feeding and, at times, appeasement after death. It travelled between the worlds of the living and the dead. The Ba survived death and was only loosely attached to the tomb. In *The Alchemy of Night* practice, according to the Prince, the heart – and

therefore the Ba – must be engaged and of good intent for the process to come to completion. When fully realised, the Ba returned to the realms of higher consciousness.

- **The Khaibit or Khabit:** the 'shadow' that was able to detach itself from the body at will and go travelling. It remained close to the Ba and the tomb after death. After death, the khaibit retained the fears and darker qualities the soul carried when in incarnation.

- **The Khu or Akhar ('the Light Body'):** the animating divine spark or 'divine intelligence'. The spiritual intelligence of the soul. An immortal, radiant being that, after death, could return to the stars and mingle with the gods. But it could still influence events on earth and, under certain circumstances, had to be appeased with appropriate offerings and rituals.

- **The Sakhu:** the incorruptible spiritual body that lived in the heavens if the soul passed the judgement of the dead. It had all the intelligence and spiritual abilities of a living being raised to a higher level.

In addition there were two other important components of a human being:

- **The Ab or Ib:** the heart. In Egyptian thought, the heart was much more than an organ that pumped blood. It was the seat of the soul and of the will and intention. It had moral awareness with the ability to make choices, good or bad. It was the Ab that was judged after death and either passed into the otherworld for eternity, or was consumed by Ammit, the soul-eater, if it failed the test, after which it totally ceased to exist.

- **The Ren:** the true name. This was kept a closely guarded secret as it was deemed a magical part of the being that had the power, in the hands of others, to obliterate the soul or to give that other the power to command the soul.

Sekhem power

The Power of Sekhem drove the whole system. It could be called 'dynamic personal power' – or the higher resonance of the kundalini force. Sekhem was the basis for *heka*, magical working. Raising the Power up the spine through the chakras to the crown brings about physical union of the male and female polarities with the divine, resulting in control over the forces of creation.

After physical death, Sekhem was perceived as an 'incorporeal personification' (that is, a subtle body or energetic net) that contained the life force of the former human being. It lived in the heavens with the Sakhu.

Chapter 3

The Alchemy in action

The Preface details the initiation of the nineteenth century finder of the ancient Prince's manuscript, Dr Paschal Beverly Randolph (P.B.R.), into the sexual mysteries, revealing how the tome came into his keeping. The ancient tome formed the basis of Randolph's system of sexual conjugation for magical purposes, set out in detail in later chapters.

The Alchemy of Night Enchiridion

Preface

The Finding

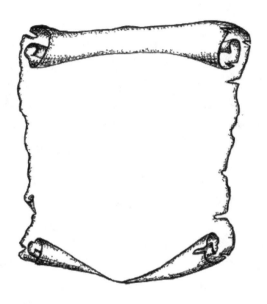

The Alchemy of Night Enchiridion

Ansairetic communication

In 1856 I had the greatest good fortune to travel throughout the Orient in search of arcane knowledge. During my travels in the wilderness of Upper Egypt, I was approached by a heavily veiled woman, beautiful of form, who showed me only her alluring walnut eyes. Following her beckoning finger, I was taken to a vast mudbrick hovel, the remnant perhaps of some ancient Pharaoh's palace that looked as though it would slide down the hillside at any moment. My dragoman was instructed to wait in the courtyard outside. As I entered through a low door, I was astounded. The "hovel" was richly furnished and I was ushered to an opulent, gold-encrusted couch and invited to sit whilst being plied with sweet fenugreek tea in delicate gold-embossed glasses served on a tray of exquisite beaten gold. An austere gentleman in Bedouin-style robes entered and nodded pleasantly towards me. After a few moments' conversation, of which I understood barely one word, he gestured around the room and the daughter, as I presumed her to be, brought forward treasures for my delectation. Ushab'tis and funeral masks, ostraca, papyri and gemstone carvings. Larger pieces of furniture and life-size statues. All were pressed upon me. When it became apparent to my host that I had but a few words of Arabic (a situation I rectified as soon as possible thereafter) my dragoman was called in to indicate that these treasures were for sale. It was with great regret that I was forced to explain that my funds were severely limited and that I was not one of the representatives of an august foreign museum such as were to be found everywhere throughout Egypt at the time.

To my surprise my host theretofore asked if I would do him the honour of spending the night in his establishment. He told me that he came from a venerable family of sand travellers, nomads who had settled over a millennium ago in the abandoned palace. When digging it out from the sand, his family had recovered many treasures – and several tombs. He wished to explain to me the origins and purpose of some of the pieces he had for sale and to have a philosophical discussion as, so he said, he could see that I was a man of culture. Deeply flattered I agreed. After passing a very pleasant evening in his company and learning much of the spiritual beliefs of the ancient peoples, I retired to the bedchamber indicated.

The reader may imagine my surprise when I awoke out of a deep sleep to find my host's daughter slipping into my bed. A full moon illuminated the room, its grey light sucking out all color but bright enough for me to luxuriate in her incandescent unveiled beauty. She communicated by gestures that I should remove the undergarments in which I slept, shrugging off her own gossamer robe. What passed between us that night introduced me to the mysteries of Ansairetic communion between a man and a woman – and the powerful spiritual entities that are the gods and goddesses themselves invoked through Affectional Alchemy. Thinking back to the discussion I had had with her father, with its veiled insinuations of almost forgotten knowledge, though of necessity circumspect as it had to pass through the lips of my dragoman, I realized I had stumbled upon a primordial tradition that had clearly been transmitted down through the ages from generation to generation within a community of initiates.

When I awoke, I found myself out on the hillside. Alone but for my dragoman. Fully clothed and clutching an ancient papyrus annotated in both demotic and Arabic script. Somehow I knew that this held the keys to the Affectional Alchemy I had experienced. I resolved to devote the remainder of my life to deciphering the text and to its promulgation – but under an edict of secrecy within mine own organisation. Those few who assisted me in the translation would never divulge its source.

This was not material for the ignorant. It took several years of painstaking translation, teaching myself the hieroglyphic and demotic languages in addition to Arabic, as I was unsure as to who else besides those few close colleagues in the organisation could be trusted with this precious information and no one had the necessary expertise. Reaching the core meaning was a challenging task indeed. But ultimately the treatise of The Prince Khem Yar Khepher'set, peace be upon him, became the foundation for my Mysteries of Eulis and the Hermetic Brotherhood of Luxor and the Great Works founded thereon.

From this nuptive experience, and my later induction into the Thaumaturgical and ansairic mysteries in Palestine and Arabia, I learned that controlled orgasm is a holy prayer that takes the initiate into an elaborate, multi-tiered and multi-dimensional cosmos that extends to the realms beyond the starry skies. It unites the two souls in conjunction with the Divine. At the moment of intense mutual orgasm – "the nuptive moment" – the souls of the partners are opened to the powers and energies of the cosmos, and anything that is truly Willed is accomplished. Love unlooses the doors of the Spirit. Ordaining power leaps from the soul like a flash of vivid white lightning, traversing space, centering on its object. This is the great magnetic Power of Love. Affectional Alchemy. The Ansairetic Mystery. The Alchemy of Night.

As exalted as are the participants at the moment of orgasm, so shall be that which enters into them from the regions above, beneath, and round about; wherefore, whatsoever male or female shall truly Will for, hopefully pray for, and earnestly yearn for, when love, pure and holy is in the nuptive ascendant, in form passional, divine and volitional, that prayer shall be granted, and the boon be given. But, as I came to realize, devout prayer must precede the moment of nuptive union, which must not be undertaken for selfish satisfaction alone as the elevated spiritual entities cannot be present other than in a joint endeavor. The ejective moment, therefore, is the most divine and tremendously important one in the human evolution as an independent entity; for not only may we launch Genius, Power, Beauty, Deformity, Crime, Idiocy, Shame or Glory on the world's great sea of Life in the person of the child we may then produce, we may plunge our own souls neck-deep in Hell's horrid slime, or else mount the Azure as coequal associate Gods; for then the mystic Soul swings wide its Golden gates, opens its portals to the whole vast Universe and through them come trooping either Angels of Light or the Grizzly Presences from the dark Corners of the Spaces. Therefore, human copulation is either ascentive and ennobling, or descensive and degrading according to how one approaches that final moment and with whom it is celebrated.

Remember, O neophyte, that GOODNESS alone is POWER. LOVE lieth at the FOUNDATION.

Dr. P.R.B.

Ohio 1868

Modern commentary

The lower form of magical child

In his reference to a child born of a union that is not of the highest soul intent, P.B.R. warns that if the intent is of a lower quality – such as pure lust or the exercise of power over another – a child so created will be of a different order than a child created from sacred union. In the modern day, this is perhaps best understood as a reference to a magical child, rather than a physical one. Not all magical creations are of the highest order of being. A 'magical child' born of uncontrolled, obsessive lust could well have malevolent or malicious intent, being a thought form that haunts the lower astral realms and seeks to interfere mischievously in the affairs of humanity, for instance.

Chapter 4

The Flames of Mut and Min

The initial chapter of the tome opens with a standard Egyptian exposition of the splitting of consciousness, or creation, into duality and opposite polarities – male and female – and the consequent creation of twinflames or 'soul mates'. There then follows an account of the needs of the soul with regard to love and the mastery of the Fires within. It briefly introduces the 'Great Central Suns', which equate to the modern day chakra system, setting the scene for the work that is to come.

The Alchemy of Night Enchiridion

I

Igniting the Flames of Min and Mut

The Alchemy of Night Enchiridion

In the Beginning

In the beginning was Quema.[1] Consciousness Was. Indivisible and divine. Within that Flame of Pure Consciousness, a young God played alone. Bored with singularity, Min made *seti* and brought the Cosmos into manifestation and duality took form. In that manifestation, two polarities were created: neither could exist without the other or the Universe would collapse into chaos.

Out of One was born the Other. All that is found in the Cosmos may be found within each individual human being, and the same principles that apply to the universe apply in the case of the individual being. Humanity was created with two sexes by the Eternal One expressly that it might commingle its masculine and feminine natures to feed the Soul. The Soul requires love in the same way as the body requires food. Each sex finds its resting place in the other. But the souls must rise above that unrest which men miscall delight. Mere sensual gratification is not the aim of the Eternal Ones. Harmony of the body reflects the heightened ecstasy and rapturous union that exists beyond the stars. Equilibrium of the Spirit Eternal arises out of mutual affinities and ecstatic meetings of Adepts with a truly spiritualised Body of Light. Erotic fulfilment without limitation is possible for such souls. But they may pay the ultimate price if separated in future lives.

Love-starvation, which is the nostalgia or homesickness of the Soul, the longing for the beloved, is the most terrible evil that can oppress the Soul. The ennui sucks the life from the Soul and thwarts humanity in its return to the stars from whence it came. Each Soul needs its complement at the Highest Level of Being. Each must seek out that which completes it and unite with the Absolute above and with the Beloved below.

* * *

Initiation commences with the mastery of the Fires within. The opening of the Central Suns and the raising of the Fires of Min and Mut[2] opens the Soul and unites it with The Eternal One. Even when the Beloved, the Twinflame, has been identified every Initiate must complete each section of the work separately but in unison. One Initiate cannot move forward until the other has simultaneously completed each stage of the Great Work. No step can be circumvented, nothing can move out of its appointed place. The Act of Will must accompany the Initiation. Desire must be controlled until the appointed time. Only then may two Adepts, recognised from birth, be conjoined in the Great Marriage and move forward in the sapient knowledge that their Souls were created to transcend Manifest Creation and return to Absolute Oneness.

* * *

The Flames of Min and Mut are the Internal Fire that ignites the sacred Flame of the Ba,[3] the Soul-bird, and leads to the Soul Unity that is Sakhu or sacerdotal union. The Flames of Min and Mut are the Soul's Love made physical. It is the love that the Soul has for the vehicle which carries it, and for its twinflame: the Soul of the Heart of the Beloved. Without the Flames of Min and Mut there can be no penetration of the veil, no merging with the Eternal One. The sacred Flames rise up the spine like entwined serpents passing through each of the Great Central Suns[4] flowering at the crown of Min, the Great Cause of Light. One Serpent, Mut, is female and soulful, an unmanifested consciousness that has the power to Be and to Manifest. The complementary Serpent, Min, is male and corporeal, dynamic, energetic and directive. It was Min, a child of the Eternal One, who single-handedly brought the physical world into being.[5] It was Min who raised up Creation out of the primal waters of the Mother's Womb. From this Flame all form was born when the Eternal One divided into male and female. The Flames are equal and opposite, polarities meeting in complementarity. As it is Above, so it is Below.

Nonetheless, the Soul in its myriad incarnations experienced masculine and feminine in all its forms. It partakes of the nature of each and Adepts must unite these two forces within their own being before making the outer marriage: sacred or profane. That unrest which men miscall delight[6] must be eschewed until the sacred joining is made. This is the Mystical Secret of the Ages. As it is Within, So it is Without, As it is Above, So it is Below. This is the only means to accomplish the miracles of the One Thing. As all things were by contemplation of the One, so all things arose from this One Thing by a Single Act of Adaptation.

Commentary

The symbolism, language and art of ancient Egyptian are polysemic, blending many levels of meaning within concepts in a way which no other language has fully mastered. Here within a primal creation story we have a clear exposition of the complementary forces that operate within the universe to hold the balance between chaos and order. We also come to appreciate how, for the ancient Egyptian, sexual activity was imbued with deeper symbolism. The creational or recreational physical act was the counterpart of a greater Renewal of Life. Masculine and feminine, positive and negative, yin and yang, Above and Below, inner and outer, God and Goddess each must be cultivated and brought into equilibrium so that the whole may be expressed and the Adept move beyond the bounds of physicality into that of union with the Spirit and spiritual fecundity. Resolution of Duality into Unity must be achieved, a fusion with the Absolute into Oneness, so that true Rejuvenation and Rebirth occurs. By this union the Adept attains liberation and enlightenment through union of the individual with the universe. The ultimate bliss of the transcendence of all dualities is the sign of the true Adept.

It is clear that the ancient Egyptians realised, as do Esotericists today, that only once the Lower Self has been mastered may the Spiritual Self be expressed and a true union of Souls brought about. They recognised that carnal desire is a potent Creationary Force but that unbridled desire leads to disaster. The personal will must be mastered first by the suppression of base sexual desire and the harnessing of the Will. It must be attached to the Will of the Soul, that Greater Being. Only then may the potency of the nuptive moment be released. In raising the Fire of Min with its entwined forces under the control of the Higher Will, the process of mastery commences. To raise the Fire, the Great Central Suns must first be opened. This is the first step to the Affectional Alchemy that unlocks the Ansairetic Mysteries. It is on this premise that I founded mine own School of the Golden Secret. A system of Alchemical and Nuptive Union. However, I fear that I shall be much misunderstood and maligned during my practice thereof. My attempts to publish have been met not only with ridicule but shall, I, with prescience suspect, result in my physical imprisonment for offences against the public morality. For this reason I endeavoured to found my School for assiduously chosen initiates who would be carefully selected for their adherence and loyalty to the deeper sacred principles embodied within these pages.

Dr. P.B.R.

Addendum notes

1   Quema is creation on many levels, a begetting in physical or spiritual form.

2   The Flames of Min and Mut are the kundalini force of the Indian continent. Two intertwining currents, one male, the other female. It is portrayed in Egyptian literature as entwined serpents on the caduceus, the staff of the magician.

3   The Ba or Soulbird is that portion of the soul said to reside in the physical heart.

4   The Great Central Suns are the seven-centred chakric system of the occultists.

5   In Egyptian creationism, Ra masturbated the world into being by the vigour of his hand but in this early recension it is the Fertility God Min who carries out the act.

6   Lower sensual gratification.

The Ansairetic system to which Dr P.B.R. refers is not at this time known to me but enquiries have been set in hand.

E.A.W.B.

Modern commentary

The creation of duality

In its original, pristine state, consciousness is one and indivisible: an integrated unity. When consciousness takes on form, and matter is created, a duality occurs through separation into component parts. The division into yin and yang, positive and negative, masculine or active (Min) and feminine or passive (Mut) begins. Duality consists of opposite and complementary poles. Neither one aspect nor the other predominates. Neither is better than the other. Nor can one aspect exist without the other or chaos would ensue. The poles balance each other, although, when in incarnation, one aspect may be more visible than the other, as with gender for instance. This duality is experienced as a separation that exists both within the external created world, the cosmos, and in the inner world, the psyche. But this is ultimately an illusion that must be dispelled.

The ancient Egyptian Hermetic alchemical principle declares 'as above, so below'. From the human perspective, integrated consciousness, or divinity, is experienced as 'above' and separated consciousness, or earthly incarnation, as 'below'. An incarnated human being perceives him or herself as an individual, yet epitomises the 'as without, so within' principle because a spark of that original consciousness remains within. That spark is nurtured and grown by following the stages of the Prince's book. Stemming from consciousness itself, when the illusion of separation is dispelled, all is one. Consciousness is all-encompassing, 'above and below, without and within'. A unity within itself. 'Absolute Oneness', as *The Alchemy of Night* puts it, is the ultimate goal of the work.

Soulmate or twinflame?

It is from this distant epoch then that we may date the innate love which human beings feel for one another, the love which restores us to our ancient state by attempting to weld two beings into one and to heal the wounds which humanity suffered.
– Plato, *The Symposium*

Plato echoes this Egyptian understanding of separation into duality, and the myth of the separation of the sky goddess Nut from her brother the earth god Geb, in his tale of how soulmates were created. In *The Symposium* he explains that human beings were originally two persons in one body, with two heads and four arms and legs. In their self-satisfied completeness, they rolled along in ecstasy, ready and able to do almost anything. These beings had formidable strength and vigour. Overweening pride led them to attack the gods. Not wanting to kill them outright, Zeus split them in half, thus diminishing both their powers and their happiness, and forcing them to spend their lives yearning for the missing half. But, if they did meet again, the outcome was not a happy one:

Each half yearned for the half from which it had been severed. When they met they threw their arms around one another and embraced, in their longing to grow together again, and they perished of hunger and general neglect of their concerns, because they would not do anything apart. When one member of a pair died and the other was left, the latter sought and embraced another partner, which might be the half either of a female whole (which is now called a woman) or a male.[13]

Plato also informs us that these original beings comprised three genders: male, female and bisexual hermaphrodites. Each male was split into two male halves, each female into two female halves, and each hermaphrodite into a male half and a female half. The male halves then sought their twin in another man, the females in another woman, and the parts from the hermaphrodite in heterosexual union. In this view, a soulmate does not necessarily have to be of a different gender. But the duality would be unbalanced unless the 'two halves' were split into a partnership where one displayed more of the active (positive) pole and the other the passive (negative), or met in perfect equilibrium. These terms are not judgemental, merely reflections of more active or passive facets being uppermost in the current incarnation. So, *The Alchemy of Night* process is equally appropriate for all types of relationship, *provided each is willing to undertake their own magical sexual and soul development individually and in tandem.*

We can glimpse in Plato's description of what happened when the two parts of one soul found each other again, one of the major pitfalls of a soulmate experience. The two halves became so enamoured of, and reliant on, each other they would perish from hunger. Soulmates can become so enmeshed and obsessed with each other that soul development becomes stultified, nothing grows. There is no forward movement.

People often describe feeling their soulmate reach out to them across the centuries. Poets are particularly good at catching this evocation of past love:

Yes, I have re-entered your olden haunts at last;
Is it really a surprise to hear me again?
Through the years, through the dead scenes I have tracked you,
Why should it be, when I have never forgotten you?
What have you now found to say of our past –
Will you not grant me one boon – to speak of that which divided us?
Scanned across the dark space therein I have lacked you?
For it is true – I have never recovered from the loss of you.
– Thomas Hardy

This kind of 'total soulmate union' can, contrary to popular belief, sometimes be totally disempowering and it may be necessary for one half to get out of the relationship in order to survive. This could well fall under the Prince's definition of a "terrible evil".

The Prince Khem Yar Khepher'set warns that two such beings could "pay the ultimate price" if separated in future lives. He states that "love-starvation", divine homesickness, is a condition that weighs heavily on the soul, "the most terrible evil". Each is drawn to seek out its complement at the highest level of being so that it may reunite and return to unity. But, he warns, rather than being lost in the other, each must complete each section of the great work of initiation separately and in unison. "Each soul needs its complement at the Highest Level of Being. Each must seek out that which completes it and unite with the Absolute above and with the Beloved below." Here is the first hint that uniting the Flames of Mut and Min may lead to something other than personal sexual satisfaction. As we will come to recognise, the mystic marriage goes way beyond the physical. The process of uniting *starts* at that level and unfolds through multidimensions, transcending 'manifest creation' and returning to 'Absolute Oneness'.

In *The Soulmate Myth*, I described twinflames as being "like soulmates but without the karma." Those who are drawn together for esoteric soulwork rather than the lessons and challenges of the everyday and whose vibrational rate matches or becomes finely attuned.

There are two types of twinflame. One in incarnation, and one outside it (the Highest Self). Rather than seeking a soulmate, in the *Enchiridion* the initiate is exhorted to seek both an incarnated twinflame with whom to complete the physical and metaphysical process, and a suprapersonal union with the twinflame that is the Highest Self. The Highest Self vibrates at a more refined rate and is an embodiment of the Absolute or divine that is outside incarnation. It is a higher vibration of the overall soul. (As we have seen, in the Egyptian view the soul has many parts.) This can perhaps best be described as union with one's own spirit – the immortal, discarnate part of oneself. The ultimate, animating spark of divinity.

Throughout this book, the term 'twinflame' will be used to describe souls drawn together to undertake such work *and* the soul union produced by aligning the physical self with the Highest Self. To draw a twinflame towards yourself, see Appendix II.

Mastering the Fires Within

The *Alchemy of Night* begins with mastering the Fires within. These Fires are the complementary polarity currents of yin and yang, male and female energies within the body. They are equivalent to the kundalini force of Indian mysticism. Two currents that lie quiescent at the base of the spine until consciously raised. However, they can rise unmediated through uncontrolled and undirected 'spiritual' activities and wreak havoc.[14] They are mediated by the 'Central Suns', equating to the chakra system of modern energy work. But the Fires are also 'the Soul's Love made physical'. Love for one's Self, the vehicle that carries the soul, *and* the Self of the 'Beloved' or physical twinflame.

The Flame of Mut is female and 'soulful', an unmanifested spark of consciousness that has the power to manifest and bring into being yet simply *Is*. It is the passive, receptive polarity. The Flame of Min is male, dynamic and directional. It is the active polarity. It was the God Min who singlehandedly, according to another version of the ancient Egyptian myth, brought the world into being. A world that then divided into duality and polarity.

The Prince emphasises that each soul will have had incarnations that encompassed both the male and female polarities. In other words, in physical or energy bodies of both genders. Not just in the physical world but also the multidimensional realms. Those polarities have to be brought into equilibrium and integrated before the mystic, or any other, marriage is made. As Randolph points out in his commentary, "for the ancient Egyptian sexual activity was imbued with deeper symbolism." It was not just a physical act. "The creational or recreational physical act was the counterpart of a greater Renewal of Life." Once the polarities were brought into equilibrium and the Power of Sekhem raised, the initiate could move beyond the bounds of physicality and duality into union with the Spirit, or overall Soul, and then to the Absolute.

Chapter 5

Opening the Central Suns

This chapter contains preparatory material outlining the role of the chakras in activating supraconsciousness. The Prince's explanation was gouged and is, therefore, partial. It is supplemented by Randolph's understanding of the chakra system as the vehicle through which divine consciousness manifests on the earth plane. According to the Prince, many weeks of concentrated practice were required to stimulate the chakras. Fortunately, in the modern world, this can be facilitated by the addition of crystals to the practice. Crystals also assist with removing 'hooks' lodged in the chakras from previous sexual encounters.

The Alchemy of Night Enchiridion

II

Opening the Secret Chambers

The Alchemy of Night Enchiridion

The Central Suns

Within the Subtle Bodies of the Sakhu, Great Suns and Secret Chambers whirl around the Central Sun of the Seat of the Heart as do the Great Divinities rotate around the Central Being of the Eternal One. The Adept who masters each of the Central Suns and activates the Secret Chambers unites the Sakhu and the Seven Soul Bodies with the Khat and shall have good health and eternal life with the Gods above and on Earth below. He will illuminate his Body of Light, so essential for survival throughout eternity. Each of the Suns and the Secret Chambers is opened by many weeks of concentrated practice with the breath, stimulating each to rotate and spiral out to join in the Great Unity Grid of Consciousness following the Celestial Starry Road of the Great Cow[1] to join the... [Commentator's note: the Papyrus is gouged at this point and resumes...]

... in this way does Below reflect Above, the miracle of the One Thing is brought forth on the Earth through the Great Central Suns and their Secret Chambers and their illuminating effect on the Body of Light.[2]

The Great Central Suns

The Anchor: Governed by the Great Sage of Wisdom Hermes and Geb the God of Earth who opens his jaws imprisoning those who are not worthy. The Anchor unites Above with Below forming a Great Chain of Being, so that the Gods may be made manifest on the Earth and the work of the Adept be brought into manifestation on the physical plane.

God's Plenty Below: Governed by the Great Green God Asar[3] the Lord of Silence and the Sky who Rose Again, He Who is

Permanently Benign and Youthful, who travels eternally with Ra amongst the Stars, and his wife the Mistress Aset, She of the Throne, Protector of the Dead whose home is in Sophet, Guardian of the Dreams and Healers, the God's Plenty Below is the source of survival for the Khat. It is where the soul bodies meet physicality. The power of this Sun must not be squandered by the unrest which men miscall delight nor may the common Will be turned towards satisfaction of mere lust. The God's Plenty Below is the source of all creativity, the primal mound of creation and the waters out of which all arose.

The Magic Eye of the Belly: Governed by the Great Mother Goddess Mut from whom the cosmos was formed in the female form, bearer of the Womb of Life, and the Great God Min the maker of Gods and men who Came Forth and for whom Pharaoh commits Seti. In the male form, this is the seat of Sekhem, soul power, and the generative force. When this Central Sun is activated the Adept may bring all being into manifestation.

The Eye of the Will: Governed by the Great God Khonsu, He Who Travels With the Moon, Watcher through the Night and Source of All Virility, where the Ka, the etheric double, takes on identify, in this Central Sun the unique personality of the incarnate being is developed through feelings, power and control. Here lies the source of the Common Will which must be mastered so that the Spiritual Will can be called forth from the Higher Realms to work in cooperation with the Divine Directive Intelligence of the Universe and manifested Below.

The Seed of the Heart: Governed by the Great Goddess Maat, Begetter of Cosmic Harmony who brought forth the Order of the Universe from chaos at the moment of creation, who holds the Point of Balance. Here, the ability to determine your destiny becomes a reality. The Seed of the Heart absorbs energy from the

Sun to stimulate the Ba's intention and drains away the noxious substances of the Khat to restore the purity of the primal waters from which creation arose.

The Seat of the Soul: Governed by The Lady Hathor the Mistress of the West and of Jubilation, Queen of the Dance, Music and Wreath Weaving, Inebriety Without End. Home of the Ba, the soulbird, and site of the identity of the soul and source of Absolute divine love.

The Voice of Divine Intelligence: Governed by The Great God Djehuti, One, Self-begotten, and Self-produced, who established the heavens, the stars, Earth and everything in them, who directs the motions of the heavenly bodies and without Whom the Gods could not exist, Knower of All, Measurer of Time, home of the Khu, the spiritual intelligence of the soul and joining place for the Body of Light.

The All Seeing Eye: Governed by The Great Lady of Wisdom Neith, mysterious and great who came to be in the beginning and caused everything to come to be. The divine mother of Ra, who shines on the horizon. The eternal virgin, indivisible, One in Herself, Personification of the primal waters and Mother of the Created World. It was the Lady Neith who wove this world into being on her loom, who told us: I am the things that are, that shall be, and that have been. No one has ever laid open the garment by which I am concealed. The fruit which I brought forth was the Sun. This Central Sun is the home of the Akhar, the divine spark, and of spiritual perspective. When this Sun opens all is revealed. The Adept can see through the veil of creation into the true being of matter, Spirit and Gods.

The Great Cause of Light: Governed by He Who Was Before All Was, Aten-Min, Director of the motions of the heavenly bodies,

First before All, home of the Sakhu, unity consciousness and the perception of The Eternal One. When this gateway is open Nuit, the Goddess of the Starry Heaven reveals herself and her milk nourishes the Earth Below.

Only when the Central Suns have come under the control of the initiate may the Body of Light be opened. Without integration into this Body the soul will wander...

... and the Body of Light is illuminated.

[Commentator's note: the papyrus is gouged out at this point as though the information has been deliberately torn away.]

Commentary

Lying along the axis of the spinal column and positioned in the Body of Light, the seven Central Suns correspond to the seven-centered chakric system outlined in Rosicrucian and Theosophical doctrine as taught to the Highest Adepts in my Brotherhood of Eulis. These are the seven major centers of the Emanation of Consciousness through which the Divine manifests on the Earth plane. The Secret Chambers of the Central Suns are the metaphysical counterpart of the major glands of the endocrine system. The Peripheral Suns equate to numerous minor chakras found in Indian and other esoteric literature.

The Adept must acquaint himself with the Secret Chambers of the Central Suns, the physical glands associated with each chakra, and with the soul parts associated with them. It would seem that the priests of antiquity believed that health and longevity would be achieved by the effect of a fully energised chakric system on the endocrine system and alignment with the soul parts. Notwithstanding, opening the Central Suns was an essential prerequisite for a Mystical Joining that would last throughout time when the chakras of two people were sacerdotally united.

Magician Priests carried the Caduceus of Hermes Trismegistus to signify that they had opened the Seven Central Suns and the numerous Peripheral Suns and harnessed them to Divine Will. Pharaoh was shown wearing the Uraeus Crown to indicate that he had reached the highest initiation of all. Indeed to become Pharaoh one must take one step beyond all others, his was the ultimate initiation, embodiment and representation of the God on Earth. His was the initiation that overcame all others, that excelled and ascended to the Highest Point.

Dr. P.B.R.

Commentary

The Egyptian Chakra System

There is little written evidence of an Egyptian chakra system and yet, with typical Egyptian subtlety, there are hieroglyphic indications as the djed pillar can in some instances represent the spine and its associated energy centres, as can the interlinked Caduceus and the *uas* staff. Notwithstanding, we can find illumination in the chakra systems of the East as concepts would have been exchanged with the merchants who travelled from Afghanistan with the precious Lapis Lazuli so sought after in Egypt. The interchange of ideas, in both directions, is visible in much of the literature for those with eyes to see it.

The Anchor: Kamrupa in the Eastern system is positioned between and beneath the feet. In the Eastern system it is not accounted as one of the major chakras but unless this chakra is functioning fully, the Adept cannot ground the spiritual life into the material world.

The God's Plenty Below: Muladhara in the Eastern system is positioned on the perineum below the last bone of the spinal column. This base chakra corresponds to the Leydig gland and the adrenals. It governs the survival of the Soul in Khat – physicality. The author warns that the power of this chakra must not be squandered through force of will in lower sensual gratification but reserved for the spiritualised fusion with the Above.

The Magic Eye of the Belly: Swadhistana in the Eastern system is positioned a hand's breadth below the navel. It will be noted that in all depictions of the God Min, his phallus is positioned at the Magic Eye of the Belly rather than the base of the belly. This sacral chakra governs the testes and ovaries and it is the source of Sekhem – soul power, the generative force. It is through this Central Sun that a deathless union with the Divine is achieved which raises the nuptive moment above erotic adventure and into an intimate ecstatic connection with the Absolute.

The Eye of the Will: Manipura in the Eastern system is positioned over the solar plexus, a hand's breadth above the navel. It governs the action of the pancreas. In the Egyptian system this was the seat of the Will, both at the lower and at the spiritual level. Mastery of this chakra enabled the Adept to control the forces beyond the physical and bend the Gods to his will.

The Seat of the Soul: Anahata in the Eastern system is positioned over the physical heart. To the Egyptians this was where the soul resided. It governs the action of the Thymus, the feelings and the emotions. Only when this chakra is fully functioning may the initiate know union with the Divine and manifest all spiritual possibilities on the Earth.

The Voice of Divine Intelligence: Vishuddha in the Eastern system is positioned over the physical throat. It governs the action of the Thyroid. It is through this chakra that the initiate expresses a direct connection with the Divine.

The All Seeing Eye: Ajna in the Eastern system is positioned on the forehead slightly above and between the eyebrows. It governs the action of the Pineal. When this chakra is functioning fully the initiate sees beyond the physical world and may access the Other Worlds and perceive the Gods themselves.

The Great Cause of Light: Sahasrara in the Eastern system is positioned at the crown of the head where the skull bones are sutured. It governs the action of the Pituitary. With this chakra open, the Adept experiences Unity Consciousness in each and every waking moment.

The Seed of the Heart: The ancient Prince accredits a further chakra, deemed minor in the Eastern system, with powerful influence in Egyptian lore, the Surya Chakra or Heart Seed. This chakra is located below the heart at the base of the breastbone above the solar plexus. Known in the East as The Wish-Fulfilling Tree, it ignites the ability to determine your destiny harnessing the Higher Will to that of the Soul. The true Seat of the Soul's Intention, it draws in heat from the sun, igniting the actions of the Manipura Chakra and the Generative Force of Creation itself. This is the linkage point for the endocrine system with the lymphatic, the great filtering system of the body and, in Egyptian philosophy, equated to the primal waters of creation.

Addendum notes

1 The Milky Way.
2 In modern metaphysical understanding, the Body of Light is the subtle etheric body that forms a vessel for the soul after death and conveys it through the Gates of Death into Eternal Life.
3 Asar is the God of the Underworld, otherwise known as Osiris, and Aset his wife Isis.
   E.A.W.B.

Modern commentary

The Egyptian Chakra system

In the Egyptian system, there are nine major chakras. Two more than in the Rosicrucian and Theosophical systems widely adopted in modern Western esoteric and metaphysical work. The additional chakras link in the higher energies of the heart and soul, soul and spirit, and ground the whole into the physical plane. Each chakra is governed by a god or goddess and the powers embodied by that god link into the subtle energy bodies that create the overall soul.

It ancient times it was believed that a well-functioning chakra system was essential for both physical and spiritual health, linking as it did to organs and glands of the physical and soul-bodies. Problems in a particular area of the body may well indicate chakra blockages that need to be cleared before the alchemy process can move forwards. In modern energy therapeutics, crystals assist these chakras to function.

The Anchor (Earth Star): Everyday reality and groundedness
Location: Beneath the feet
Soul-body connection: Khaibit
Soul-consciousness: Material, corporeal
Physiology: Physical body, electrical and meridian systems, sciatic nerve and sensory organs.
Crystals: Eye of the Storm (Judy's Jasper), Flint, Graphic Smoky Quartz, Hematite, Serpentine Smoky Quartz, Smoky Quartz Elestial.

This chakra is connected to the Earth god, Geb, and the male principle. It is concerned with security and survival issues. The function of the Anchor is to link the spiritual energies of 'above' into the physical plane 'below'. Unless this chakra is functioning optimally, the initiate cannot ground the alchemical process into the everyday world. The Anchor connects you to the Earth's core energy source in addition to its electromagnetic fields and energetic meridians. This chakra helps you to bring things into concrete form, grounding and earthing new frequencies and actualising plans and dreams into physical manifestation. It is a place of safety and regeneration. If it is not activated, you will have only a toehold in incarnation and will be physically and psychologically ungrounded. With it functioning well, you have a stable, calm and strong centre into which to assimilate the Power of Sekhem – the sexual and spiritual life-force. If your Anchor is not functioning, you will be unable to assimilate and ground the Power of Sekhem when it is awakened. When the chakra is functioning at optimum, you have a natural physical and spiritual energy circuit.

God's Plenty Below (Base chakra): Basic instincts and survival
Location: Base of the perineum
Soul-body connection: Khat
Soul-consciousness: Instinctual will
Physiology: 'Fight or flight' response, adrenals, bladder, elimination systems, gonads, immune system, kidneys, lower back, lower extremities, sciatic nerve, lymph system, prostate gland, rectum, skeletal system, veins.
Crystals: Fire Agate, Jasper, Kundalini Quartz, Onyx, Poppy Jasper, Red Carnelian, Red Garnet, Red Triplite, Red Zincite, Ruby, Serpentine.

The God's Plenty Below is ruled by Osiris (Asar), god of fertility and resurrection and by Isis (Aset), goddess of healing and magic. It is where the energy of the subtle Khat conjoins with the physical body and where soul-bodies meet in sexual congress. This chakra is the source of creativity and procreation. The God's Plenty is linked to your core energy, your 'root support' and connection to Earth. It is the foundation for all the other chakras along the spine, a secure base on which they rest. It represents both your home and your place in the world. When it functions optimally, you are grounded and connected to your core. It is where the Power of Sekhem force lies curled around your etheric tailbone, the sacrum or 'sacred bone', before it is awakened. The base chakra is also the site of the will to survive and the ability to make thing happen. This is where you discover yourself as an individual and take responsibility for yourself. When this chakra is functioning well, you trust the universe. Imbalances here lead to sexual disturbances and feelings of stuckness, anger, impotence and frustration – and inability to let go.

The Magic Eye of the Belly (Sacral chakra): Core energy management

Location: Below the navel

Soul-body connection: Sekhem Power

Soul-consciousness: Generative, primal will

Physiology: Bladder and gallbladder, immune and elimination systems, kidneys, large and small intestines, lumbar and pelvic region, sacrum, spleen, ovaries, testes, uterus.

Crystals: Fire Opal, Kundalini Quartz, Mookaite Jasper, Orange Carnelian, Orange Scheelite, Orange Sphalerite, Zincite.

The Magic Eye is governed by the great Mother Goddess Mut from whom the cosmos was formed, bearer of the Womb of Life, and the great god Min. This is the seat of Sekhem, soul power, the passionate generative force. This creative chakra is an important part of your core energy system and your ability to bring things into manifestation. It also assists you to hold your boundaries steady. It is allied to how you handle your immediate environment and matters such as authority figures. When this chakra is working well, you experience yourself as a dynamic agent of change. If it is blocked, you cannot experience yourself as a potent sexual being, causing feelings of impotence and powerlessness, or overwhelming lustful urges. The Magic Eye affects how easily you express your sexuality and how you feel about relationships. It may also hold on to parenting issues and the connection to your family and the ancestral source. Imbalances here lead to infertility and blocked creativity at all levels.

One of the 'pleasure chakras', the Magic Eye enlivens life by stimulating the production of endorphins and 'feel good' hormones. With this chakra functioning well, you are able to give and receive in equal measure. Without it, you are shut off from nurturing and sharing, becoming jealous and possessive.

The Magic Eye is where 'hooks' from other people may make themselves felt, particularly from previous sexual encounters. Such hooks require clearing before the *Alchemy of Night* can take place (see page 77).

The Eye of the Will (Solar plexus chakra): Emotional knowing

Location: Solar plexus

Soul-body connection: Ka and psyche

Soul-consciousness: Emotional will

Physiology: Adrenals, digestive system, liver, lymphatic system, metabolism, muscles, pancreas, skin, small intestine, stomach, eyesight.

Crystals: Celtic Golden Healer, Citrine, Golden Healer Quartz, Grape Chalcedony, Prairie Tanzanite, Topaz, Yellow Jasper.

The Eye of the Will is governed by the Great God Khonsu, Source of All Virility. This Eye is where the Ka, the etheric double, takes on identity. The unique personality of an incarnate being is developed through feelings, power and control. The everyday will, seated here, has to be mastered and transformed so that the spiritual will can manifest. The solar plexus represents radiant self-confidence and self-esteem – and has a powerful effect on your ability to assert yourself. The Eye is where you store emotions and it can have a profoundly psychosomatic effect. It is where you assimilate nourishment, an idea or an emotion. It is also where you can take on energy and emotions from outside yourself. If not appropriately protected, this can lead to emotional overwhelm. Functioning well, it acts as a point of equilibrium between your present soul purpose and your past karma, creating emotional stability. It is also the seat of 'gut instincts' and bodily knowing. Manipulative emotional 'hooks' from other people may be located here.

The Seed of the Heart (Heart Seed chakra): Soul intention
Location: Over the xiphoid process, at the tip of breastbone
Soul-body connection: Khu (Akh)
Soul-consciousness: Multidimensional spiritual will
Physiology: Integrated physical and subtle energy systems.
Crystals: Anandalite, Azeztulite, Brandenberg Amethyst, Iolite
    with Sunstone, Orange Sphalerite, Tugtupite.

Governed by the Great Goddess Maat, Begetter of Cosmic Harmony, the Seed of the Heart helps you to recall your reason for incarnation. Opening this chakra connects you to your soul purpose and reveals how it fits into the overall divine plan. Here, the ability to determine your destiny becomes a reality. The Seed drains away toxic energies to restore soul purity, absorbing cosmic energy from the Sun to stimulate the Ba's intention. When the Heart Seed is functioning optimally it connects the lightbody and multidimensional consciousness to your soul.

The Seat of the Soul (Heart chakra): Unconditional love and
    compassion
Location: Centre of the chest
Soul-body connection: Ba and Ib
Soul-consciousness: Self-awareness
Physiology: Chest, circulation, heart, lungs, shoulders, thymus,

respiratory system.

Crystals: Emerald, Green Aventurine, Malachite, Mangano Calcite, Peridot, Rose Quartz, Ruby in Kyanite, Tugtupite.

Governed by The Lady Hathor, the Seat of the Soul carries the identity of the soul. It is the core of your being: where the physical and the spiritual energies fuse and unconditional love thrives and is shared with others. It is the site of bonds made with other people, your relationships, and your interaction with the wider worlds around you. When the Seat of the Soul is open, you 'live from your heart' feeling safe and compassionate. There is no judgement in an open heart chakra. This is the basis of unconditional respect for others. The Seat of the Soul is also the site of unselfish self-love. If you cannot love and accept yourself, then you cannot love others or receive their love. Self-love helps you to rise above egotism and asserts your self-worth. This chakra is a connection centre that integrates the whole line of chakras along the spine. It helps you to realise that you are part of a much larger picture and opens the way to higher knowledge.

The Voice of Divine Intelligence (Throat chakra): Communication

Location: Throat

Soul-body connection: Ren

Soul-consciousness: Universal mind

Physiology: Ears, nose, respiratory and nervous systems, sinuses, skin, throat, thyroid, parathyroid, tongue, tonsils, speech and body language, metabolism.

Crystals: Blue Calcite, Blue Lace Agate, Eilat Stone, Kyanite, Lapis Lace Onyx, Septarian, Sodalite, Turquoise.

Governed by The Great God Djehuti (Thoth), Knower of All, Measurer of Time, the Voice of Divine Intelligence communicates the spiritual intelligence of the soul. It is where you express yourself, including strongly felt feelings and emotions that come from the heart or solar plexus chakra as well as thoughts. When it is functioning optimally, you make yourself heard. When it is not, misunderstandings and inappropriate compromises arise. This chakra has a surprising amount to do with willpower and the choices that arise in life as it mediates contact with the external world.

The All Seeing Eye (Third Eye): Metaphysical sight and insight

Location: Centre of forehead, between and above the eyes
Soul-body connection: Khu-Akhar
Soul consciousness: Intuitive multidimensional awareness
Physiology: Brain, ears, eyes, neurological and endocrine systems, pineal and pituitary glands, hypothalamus, production of serotonin and melatonin, temperature control, scalp, sinuses.
Crystals: Amethyst, Apophyllite, Aquamarine, Azurite, Bytownite, Flint, Labradorite, Lapis Lazuli, Moonstone, Preseli Bluestone, Rhomboid Selenite.

Governed by The Great Lady of Wisdom Neith, who caused everything to come to be, this chakra is the home of the Akhar, the divine spark, and of spiritual perspective. When this chakra opens, all is revealed. You see through the veil of creation into the true nature of matter, Spirit and Gods. The brow chakra is where your inner sight meets your outer sight and bonds into intuitive insight. It assists in seeing beyond consensual reality into what truly is. Imbalances here open you to bombardment by other people's thoughts, or irrational intuitions that have no basis in truth. Controlling or coercing mental 'hooks' from other people may lock in and affect your thoughts. There will be a greater awareness of auras and chakras, but discretion is needed to ensure that the chakra really is functioning at optimum and not acting on wishful thinking and illusion.

If you develop a headache or migraine (common when this chakra is first opening up) during psychic work, open the chakra with Apophyllite or Rhomboid Selenite. If dizziness results, push the energy down to your feet, or close the chakra down with Flint or Preseli Bluestone until you can adjust your energies appropriately.

The Great Cause of Light (Crown chakra): Multidimensional connection

Location: Top of head

Soul-body connection: Sakhu

Soul consciousness: Unity consciousness

Physiology: Brain, central nervous system, hair, hypothalamus, pituitary gland, spine, subtle energy bodies, cerebellum, nervous motor control, posture and balance.

Crystals: Anandalite™, Azeztulite, Blue Kyanite, Brandenberg Amethyst, Eye of the Storm (Judy's Jasper), Petalite, Quartz.

Governed by Aten-Min, He Who Was Before All Was, this chakra is the centre for unity consciousness and perception of the divine. When this gateway is open Nuit, the Goddess of the Starry Heaven and the female principle, reveals herself and her milk nourishes the Earth Below. An exceedingly powerful energy vortex, the crown chakra is the place of spiritual, intellectual and intuitive *knowing* so that you understand what is around you on many levels. It connects to multidimensions and multiverses. When the Power of Sekhem reaches the crown chakra it opens transcendent knowing. However, if the flow is not controlled the energy fountains out rather than flowing in a great cyclical circuit back to 'below'. When the crown chakra is blocked, you are disconnected from your spiritual self and from cosmic energies. Spiritual interference may result and metabolic or psychological imbalances are common.

Opening the Earth Star and the grounding root

Before progressing further, practise opening your Earth Star chakra and establishing a grounding root to 'below'. This is an essential part of alchemical initiation. Keeping your Earth Star chakra open and grounded into the centre of the planet helps you to be comfortable in incarnation and facilitates assimilation of higher dimensional and alchemical energies into the physical plane. The simplest way to open this chakra is with a visualisation assisted by a crystal:

- Stand or sit with your feet slightly apart, well balanced on your knees and hips. Feet flat on the floor.
- Place a Flint, Eye of the Storm (Judy's Jasper), Graphic Smoky Quartz, Hematite, Smoky Quartz, Smoky Quartz Elestial or other grounding stone between your feet.
- Picture the Earth Star chakra about a foot beneath your feet opening like the petals of a water lily.
- Place your hands over your belly, fingers touching, just below your navel. Spread your fingers so that the whole belly is covered.
- Feel roots growing from your fingers and spreading out to your hips.
- At your hips, the roots twine together and make their way down your thighs.
- Pause at your knees. Put your hands over your knees and intuitively check out how the energy feels. If the area is 'dead' and lifeless, or if the energy is whirling rapidly, place Flint or Charoite on your knees until the energy stabilises.
- Continue picturing the roots passing through your knees, down your calves, into your ankles and into the soles of your feet.
- Feel the two roots growing from the soles of your feet to meet in the Flint. Here they twist together to form one root.

- The root then passes into the Earth Star, going deep into the earth. It passes through the outer mantle, down past the solid crust and deep into the molten magma.
- When the entwined root has passed through the magma, it reaches the big iron crystal ball at the centre of the planet.
- The root hooks itself around this ball, holding you firmly in incarnation and helping you to be grounded and anchored.
- Energy and protection can flow up this root to keep you energised and safe. Or toxic energies can be passed down the root into the magma for transmutation.
- Allow the connection to pass up from the Earth Star through your feet, up your legs and knees and into your hips. At your hips, the roots move across to meet in the base chakra and from there to the sacral and the dantien – a power point sited just below your navel. The energy that flows up from the centre of the Earth can be stored in the dantien until required.

Chakra hooks

Chakra blockages can arise from a variety of causes, creating either a slow or too rapid 'spin' of the links between the chakras, the physical and the subtle bodies. One of the major reasons for blockages is that of 'hooks', lodged in the chakra, created by energetic remnants and memories of previous sexual encounters. Every prior sexual and emotional encounter will have left its imprint, no matter how fleeting *whether at a physical or subtle level*. The sexual act does not have to be physical – as *The Alchemy of Night* novel demonstrates only too well. Few people realise how powerful a lustful thought or an emotional yearning can be. It hooks into the chakra leaving a 'what if' thought-form behind it. Fortunately a crystal quickly removes these hooks and restores the correct spin speed to a chakra so that it functions at optimum. The Power of Sekhem then flows unimpeded up the chakric line.

Opening and purifying the chakras

Once the root is in place, the next stage is to open and purify each of the chakras in turn. This is quickly achieved with the assistance of a crystal. A Lemurian Seed crystal wand is ideal for this process, or you could use a long Quartz point or Selenite Wand. Remember to cleanse the crystal before beginning (*see Appendix I*).

- Starting at your feet, spiral the crystal out from the chakra and away. (Go in the direction the crystal wants to take your hand, don't force it.)
- Cleanse the crystal (*see Appendix I*).
- Spiral back into the chakra in the opposite direction.
- Move upwards through all the chakras until you've opened and purified as far as the crown.

Alternatively

If you are fortunate enough to have an Anandalite™ crystal, then the chakras can be rapidly cleansed and stabilised using this divine-light-bringing stone. You may need the assistance of a friend to complete the exercise. Remember to cleanse the crystal afterwards (*see Appendix I*).

- Starting at the floor in front of your feet, sweep the crystal up through the chakras, going from front to back, passing high over your head. Allow the crystal to lead the way and to choose how far away from the body it needs to be. If the crystal slows down or stops, wait until it is ready to move again.
- Touch the floor at the back and then reverse the process, going up and over the head down to the floor in front of you.

- Now sweep from side to side, and back again.

See also Tie cutting and partnership-contract dissolution, Appendix IV.

Drawing energy through the chakras

Once the chakras have been opened and purified, practise drawing earth energy up from 'below' (the Earth Star) to 'above' (the crown chakra) and then returning it to the base to begin the cycle again. You could draw it up the front of the body and down the back. However, drawing it up your central line and then letting it flow back down and around your auric field sets up an energetic pattern that you will be using later. Placing an appropriate crystal at your feet and over your base chakra assists the raising process. Once you are comfortable with the process, incorporate light from 'above' into the process.

- Switch off your phone and ensure you will not be disturbed.
- Stand comfortably with your knees loose and your hips balanced over them. Be aware of your grounding root anchoring you to the planet.
- Take your attention down to your feet. You could place a Hematite or Flint crystal here. As you breathe deeply into your belly, picture energy rising from the core of the planet into the Earth Star and then up your grounding root and into your base chakra.
- As you breathe out, hold the energy in the base chakra by clenching your buttocks and pulling in the lower belly. To assist, hold a Kundalini Quartz, Triplite, Poppy Jasper or Serpentine crystal over the chakra. As you breathe in, pull the energy from the base chakra to the sacral. Move the base chakra crystal upwards.
- As you breathe out, hold the energy in the sacral chakra,

pulling in the belly and clenching your buttocks as you do so.

- Continue working up through the chakras, clenching and holding the energy at each point as you breathe out, until you reach the crown.
- Breathe in, pulling the energy up to the crown where it connects to 'above'.
- As you breathe out, let the energy fall gently down your back or around the outside of your auric field until it reaches the Earth Star once more.
- Begin the circulation process again.
- Repeat for 7–10 rounds.[15]

As you continue to practise, you will find that it becomes easier to *feel* the energy rising up through the chakras and circulating back to the Earth Star. Once you can pull the energy up at will simply by thinking about it – i.e. imagining it – you are ready to move on to the next stage of the process.

Infusing the chakras with the energy of 'above'

This is a preparatory exercise, the effect of which will become much more potent as you move through the stages of initiation into the mystic marriage. It opens two further chakras, high vibration portals located above the head, and one below the Earth Star linking to the soul of Mother Earth 'below'. In ancient Egyptian drawings, the higher chakras are indicated by the horns of Hathor, the stepped headdress of Isis, the cannabis leaf that sits above Seshat's head and the sun-and-serpent headdress that adorns so many images of the divine ones.

The higher chakras

'Higher' chakras are a matter of resonance and frequency, an energy refinement not a judgement. The Gaia Gateway chakra, for instance, is a higher resonance of the Earth Star, that is, it connects to the soul of the planet and grounds spirit from 'above' and is essential for anchoring *The Alchemy of Night*. The higher crown chakras include the Soul Star and the Stellar Gateway but there are many more higher vibration chakras above the head, going way up through exceedingly high vibrations, multidimensions and multiverses. These additional chakras will automatically open up as *The Alchemy of Night* process progresses. It is essential to have fully grounded and integrated all the chakras below, up to and including the Stellar Gateway before these exceedingly high vibration chakras can be safely activated. Above the Stellar Gateway, the highest chakras become a dimension in themselves rather than an energy vortex that is more or less restricted to a four-dimensional realm.

The Gaia Gateway: Sphere of anchoring Light

Location: Approximately an arm's length beneath your feet, below the Earth Star, although it may be much deeper into the planet

Sphere of consciousness: Earth's subtle soul energy

Soul body connection: Links to the soul of the planet.

Gaia Gateway chakra crystals: Apache Tear, Basalt, Black Calcite, Black Flint, Black Kyanite, Black Spot Herkimer Diamond, Day and Night Quartz, Fire and Ice, Jet, Master Shamanite, Mohawkite, Morion, Naturally Dark Smoky Quartz (not irradiated), Nebula Stone, Nirvana Quartz, Nuummite, Petalite, Preseli Bluestone, Rainbow or Sheen Obsidian, Shungite, Smoky Elestial Quartz, Snowflake Obsidian, Spider Web Obsidian, Stromatolite, Tektite, Tibetan Black Spot Quartz, Tourmalinated Quartz.

The Gaia Gateway anchors high frequency light into the physical body and the body of the Earth. Without this chakra, high vibrational energy cannot be assimilated and grounded. It adjusts your biomagnetic frequency so that it remains in harmonic resonance with that of the planet *and* facilitates an uplift in your own personal resonance and that of the earth. It, together with the Stellar Gateway, allows the Power of Sekhem energy to travel up the spine, into the higher chakras over the head, and then to cascade down through the subtle energy bodies into the Gaia Gateway. The energy then travels back up to the dantien (the power point just below the navel) where it can be stored until needed, or moved out in the cells and intercellular spaces of the physical and subtle bodies. The chakra connects you to the soul and spirit of the planet, Gaia, and to Mother Earth herself. When your Gaia Gateway is open and functioning at optimum, you are aware of being a part of a sacred whole, part of the energy system of the Earth and, at the same time, Absolute Oneness. By holding you gently in incarnation and in contact with the soul of the planet, it mitigates the more extreme symptoms of uncontrolled kundalini and the Power of Sekhem rise.[16]

The Soul Star: Sphere of ultimate soul awareness

Location: About a foot above your head

Sphere of consciousness: An interface with the universe, the soul and Self, and all that lies beyond

Soul-body connection: The Khu (Akhar)

Soul Star crystals: Ajoite, Amethyst Elestial, Amphibole, Anandalite, Angel's Wing Calcite, Apophyllite, Auralite 23, Azeztulite, Blue Flint, Brandenberg Amethyst, Celestite, Chevron Amethyst, Citrine, Danburite, Diaspore (Zultanite), Elestial Quartz, Fire and Ice, Golden Enhydro Herkimer, Golden Himalayan Azeztulite, Green Ridge Quartz, Hematite, Herkimer Diamond, Kunzite, Kyanite, Lapis Lazuli, Lavender Quartz, Merkabite Calcite, Natrolite, Nirvana Quartz, Novaculite, Nuummite, Orange River Quartz, Petalite, Phenacite, Rainbow Mayanite, Rosophia, Satyamani and Satyaloka Quartz, Scolecite, Selenite, Shungite, Spirit Quartz, Stellar Beam Calcite, Sugilite, Tangerine Aura Quartz,

Tanzanite, Tanzine Aura Quartz, Titanite (Sphene), Trigonic Quartz, Vera Cruz Amethyst, White Elestial Quartz.

The Soul Star acts as a bridge between spirit and matter. A linkage point for the Highest Self and the point where the soul transcends the ego. This chakra adjusts extremely high spiritual frequencies so they can be integrated into matter. When assimilated by the physical body, the higher vibration resonances can be expressed here on Earth.

The Stellar Gateway: Cosmic doorway to other worlds
Location: Above the Soul Star
Sphere of consciousness: Multidimensional awareness and the
  multiverses. Connection to Absolute Oneness
Soul-body connection: The Sakhu
Stellar Gateway crystals: Ajoite, Amethyst Elestial, Amphibole,
  Anandalite™, Angel's Wing Calcite, Apophyllite, Azeztulite,
  Blue Kyanite, Brandenberg Amethyst, Celestite, Diaspore
  (Zultanite), Elestial Quartz, Golden Himalayan Azeztulite,
  Golden Selenite, Green Ridge Quartz, Kunzite, Merkabite
  Calcite, Moldavite, Nirvana Quartz, Novaculite, Petalite,
  Phenacite, Stellar Beam Calcite, Titanite (Sphene), Trigonic
  Quartz, White Elestial Quartz.

The Stellar Gateway is a dimensional portal rather than a physical site. It is a point of connection to the divine and to the multiverses surrounding us. This portal is where the soul can make a connection to its own highest self, moving through other realms, multidimensions and Absolute Oneness. When functioning optimally, spiritual illumination results and the Power of Sekhem reaches its highest manifestation.

Higher chakra activation
This activation should be carried out once the basic chakras

along the spine have been purified and opened. Repeat the purification process before activating the higher chakras. Do not rush. Open one at a time and give that chakra time to integrate into your entire chakra system before moving on to the next one. Allow yourself at least a week and probably longer to open and fully integrate the higher chakras. Do this before attempting to activate the Power of Sekhem. Remember to open all the chakras up to the new chakra before beginning each fresh activation.

Higher Chakra activation stages

This exercise is best carried out lying down as it facilitates placing the crystals and helps you to remain grounded.

- Ensure that your grounding root (page 75) is in place.
- Consciously open the chakras from the Earth Star up and along the spine to the crown. You can use the power of your imagination or a crystal to activate these.
- Place a large Smoky Elestial, Hematite, Flint or other grounding stone below your feet to anchor the energies and a Selenite or Anandalite™ crystal over your head.
- Place a Gaia Gateway chakra crystal (see page 83) on the Gaia Gateway and feel it connect to the Earth Star to anchor all your energetic bodies to the planet.
- Place a high vibration crystal such as Selenite, Anandalite™ (Aurora Quartz), Rainbow Mayanite or Azeztulite on the Soul Star to connect to your soul and Highest Self. Invoke your Highest Self to guard the chakra. Be aware of this chakra's connection to the Earth Star. Remember to close the chakra when not in use.
- Before opening the Stellar Gateway, invoke a guardian spirit or other protective being to guard it. Place Selenite, Anandalite, Phenacite, Rainbow Mayanite or other Stellar Gateway crystal to open the portal.
- Breathe in deeply through the crown of your head, feel

the divine energies of light flooding through the higher chakras and into your crown.

- Draw that light right down to the Earth Star at your feet, filling each chakra, breathing deeply and rhythmically as you do so.
- Be aware of the Soul Star's connection to the Earth Star beneath your feet and feel the energies connecting around the outside of your subtle energy bodies to create an energetic circuit.
- Draw the light on down to your Gaia Gateway. Be aware of the Stellar Gateway chakra's connection to the Gaia Gateway and feel the energies connecting around the outside of your subtle energy bodies to create an energetic circuit.
- When the process is complete, take your hands to the Heart Seed chakra to connect to your soul with these higher chakras.
- Remember to close each higher chakra portal when an activity is complete and to re-establish your grounding cord.

Chapter 6

Raising the Fire of Mut (the female Flame)

This chapter is for female initiates, anyone occupying a body of male gender should turn to the next chapter. Here preparations to raise The Power of Sekhem begin with raising the female Flame. It should only be undertaken once all the chakras are open and purified as otherwise the energy deflects tangentially from its course, which may have unpleasant consequences. The instructions to bathe and wear clean clothes are recommended for all future stages as they are an integral part of magical preparation. It may take a certain amount of practice to achieve this orgasmic raising to the brink seven times without going over the edge. Seven was the magical number of completion and perfection in ancient Egypt. The ultimate orgasm.

The Alchemy of Night Enchiridion

III

Raising the Fire of Mut

The Alchemy of Night Enchiridion

Raising the female Flame

As the Great Goddess revivified her husband and brought forth her Son, so will the female Adept raise the Fire of Mut to bring forth the spiritual Fire within. As the Womb of the Goddess was the primal waters from out of which all creation arose, so will the female Fire return the Soul to its Source in the Above.

Having bathed and purified the body with salt and incense, the initiate must first anoint the Great Central Suns with Oil of Blue Lotus[1] in a circular motion following the Great Sun God from east to west and through the Gates of Night to greet the dawn and salute the rising God once more. Stand with feet apart facing the Great God. Keep the feet planted firmly on the Earth. Listen to the heart beat within, to the Soul fluttering softly within the body. With each beat rotate the hips first to the front, then to the right hand side, to the back and to the left hand side seven times. Reverse the direction and rotate for seven more circles. Wait. Breathe.

* * *

The gateway to the sacred Fire is opened.

* * *

The initiate then lies down in a cool, dark place. The most powerful time being in the evening after the fall of twilight as Ra fights his enemies in the Underworld, or with the dawn as Ra rises triumphant again. To raise the sacred Fire, stimulate the kat, the God's Plenty Below[2], in whatever way is most effective. A Ben Ben[3] may utilised or prestidigitation. The instant the Fire begins to burn, hold as still as a gazelle when beheld by the jackal. As it fades, begin stimulation again. Repeat two more times.

Rest the left hand against the pudenda, the mound of Mut, with the middle digit[4] extending over the clitoris into the God's Plenty Below. Place the right hand above it. With the tip of the third finger stimulate the kat until the waves of sacred Fire begin to burn. As the flames rise, engage the middle finger to stimulate the length and then base of the clitoris. Breathe in deeply, pull back the belly, and allow the sacred Fire to flow into the Great Central Sun at the base of the spine and to rise like a serpent up the spinal column opening the Secret Eye of the Belly, twining upwards and lighting up each of the Great Central Suns. When it reaches the heart it stimulates the Seat of the Soul which entwines with the Fire of Min to stimulate the Secret Chambers of the Central Suns. With every breath the Fire rises ever higher until it reaches the Gate of Min[5] and the Great Cause of Light above the head.

Once the raising of the Fire has been mastered, as the Adept exhales long and slow, the Fire cascades down through the body, arms and hands and meets the God's Plenty Below. The Fire becomes a great circle uniting the Khat, material body, the Ba Soulbird, and the Great God. Cascading through the whole of the Adept's being, it animates the *Khu*, bringing the Great Body of Light closer to infuse the *ka* and the whole of the physical and spiritual being. So below, as above. The Neters are brought to the Earth and the Adept closer to the Heavens.

Repeat until the Fire has been lit seven times. The Adept may truly say: "I am the embodiment of the Goddess. I am become Divine." Once this is achieved, the Adept may use the power of the heart to master and direct the Fire to circle in and store it beneath the navel in the Cave of Min.[6]

* * *

Practice over the course of several weeks may be required before the sacred Fire can be lit seven times, the full body irradiated with the orgasmic force and the Secret Chambers of the Central Suns fully activated. Once this occurs, taking the attention up through the body as the orgasm progresses unites heart and mind, body and soul with the divine force and facilitates control by the higher will over the process.

Once true mastery has been achieved, the orgasmic force can be raised purely by The Power of Sekhem itself. It is seen in the Eye of the Mind and the force rises of its own volition and Will. The Adept is then ready to unite with the forces of Min.

Notwithstanding, a greater secret will the Adept discover once the generative power is under control. It is a matter of Will and yet something beyond the Will. The Great Magnetic Power of Love can be joined to Desire and Intent. These powers when combined can be accumulated and projected over a vast distance to attract a new Love. A Companion of the Heart. A Twinflame throughout Eternity. Such a One may be found by gazing at the image in a magic mirror and attracted by projecting the power into a ring to be worn on the Hathor, Heart, Finger or an amulet...

[Translator's note: the papyrus is broken off at this point.]

Commentary

If the female is to engage fully in the process of raising the Sacred Flame certain preparations are of necessity to be undertaken alone or in a sisterhood if a properly inaugurated esoteric group is available. Working with the untrained may raise issues of jealousy arising out of uncontrolled magnetism and improper attraction. In such cases, it is better to work alone following the instructions given.

In ancient times the Adept would be carefully prepared by her older sisters within the temple in a room and with tools consecrated for that purpose. The Papyrus of Mut sets out the tools and the guidance to be followed step by careful step until the power is raised and may be directed by an act of will to flow entwined with the male and the power of Min during sexual congress.

In addition to raising the female Fire, this ritual activates the subtle endocrine system linking the glands in the physical body to those in the subtle, soul body. This dramatically increases health, longevity and well-being on all levels.

It is clear from my research that woman must place herself in control of her soul as well as her body. Her mind, purpose, thought, desire, intent and destination must become One. In that tender state she instantly becomes an attracting power drawing to her Mate. This is the Great Magnetic Power of Love to which the ancient Prince refers. It is unfortunate that his recipe for charging an object with magnetic force is lost. One can only surmise that such a power may have survived across the centuries pulling together two souls across the aeons as happened to myself. 'La Blondette', that cool, conscienceless, sinister, thin-lipped, blue-eyed affectional sorceress, pursued me across the centuries. Of her I can write no more here but let it be a warning to the reader. Without the guidance of the sacred wisdom such relationships may fail.

The ancient Prince identified the falling and rising of the Sun God as the time of maximum potency. In my extensive research, however, any time in the evening or between three and eight of the clock in the morning shall suffice. If working with a partner, as men are more powerful in the morning, a joining will be more easily achieved between the hours of six and eight.

Dr. P.B.R.

Addendum notes

1   Oil of Blue Lotus is a rare substance in these modern times. Good quality Oil of Damascene Rose may be substituted.

2   The kat or God's Plenty Below is the vulva or yoni and the clitoris.

3   A Ben Ben is the Shiva Lingam or stone phallus of Eastern Philosophy.

4   The Egyptians believed that the vena amoris (the vein of love) ran directly from the tip of the third finger of the left hand to the heart, the seat of the soul.

5   The Gate of Min relates to the chakras above the crown.

6   The Cave of Min sits above the Sacral Chakra. It is the Dantien of Eastern Philosophy, storage point for the revivifying Lifeforce.

E.A.W.B.

Modern commentary

Female initiation

This is where the female initiate moves deep into the process of *The Alchemy of Night,* stirring the physical sexual force (the Fire of Mut) into being and bringing it up the spine so that the act of self-pleasuring becomes mastery of spiritual unity with the divine. The Fire of Mut is a slightly lower vibration of the psycho-spiritual force that is the Power of Sekhem, which is raised once the Fire of Mut has been mastered. The exercise should follow a short period of abstinence and chakra purification.

Preparation

Prepare your space carefully. Bathe in warm water that has rose oil and Halite or Himalayan salt added. Put on a robe or fresh clothes. Burn appropriate candles and anoint yourself with good-quality Attar of Roses if Oil of Blue Lotus is not available. The use of raising and controlling crystals ensures that the Flame will not rise in an uncontrolled fashion or shoot off at a tangent rather than smoothly rising up the spine. Ensure that you will not be disturbed as each step should lead seamlessly into the next.

Timing

The Prince identifies sunrise and sunset as the optimum time for this rite. P.B.R. suggests that any time in the evening or between three and eight o'clock in the morning would be appropriate. But see also the ultradian rest-phase cycle on page 12, which could identify the best time for you.

Step 1: Anointing the chakras

- Beginning with the base chakra and, using a circular

movement, with a fingertip rub a little of the oil into each chakra in turn, using whichever motion feels right for you. Breathe deeply into your belly as you do so, taking the fragrance deep within yourself. As you breathe out, feel the energy beginning to rise to the next chakra.

- Continue the process until all the chakras have been anointed.

Step 2: The activating movements

A shamanic drum heart-rhythm assists this stage.

- Stand with your feet apart, facing south.
- Pause for a moment and listen to the beat of your heart.
- With each beat, move your hips to the rhythm. First to the front, then out to the right-hand side, to the rear, and across to the left and then back to the resting position. Move the remainder of your body as little as possible.
- Repeat seven times.
- Then reverse the direction.
- Standing quietly, breathe gently. Feel the gateway at the base of the spine opening, the Fire of Mut waiting to rise.

Step 3: Raising the Sacred Flame

- Lie down in a quiet, candlelit room.
- Ensure that your grounding root is in place.
- Place a raising crystal at your feet or over your base chakra.
- Take your attention to the top of your head and feel the higher chakras opening and pouring light down through your chakras to your feet. Breathe the energy in deeply, anchoring it to the Earth Star.
- Place a Power of Sekhem controlling crystal over your head to direct the flow.
- Stimulate your vagina and clitoris in whatever way you

prefer, either with fingers or with a Shiva Lingam (using a vibrator may well take you over the edge too soon), but stop the moment you begin to feel totally aroused and on the brink. This awakens the Fire. Do not come to orgasm. Hold still. Repeat twice more. From here on, rhythmically contracting the vagina in harmony with your breathing assists the process.

- Place your hand at the base of your belly, resting your fingers on the clitoris and vulva. (The Prince suggested using the left hand as this was believed to connect directly to the heart.)
- Rest the right hand lightly over the left to create a circuit.
- Extend your middle finger into the vagina and, with the tip of the third finger, stimulate the clitoris until orgasm rises, stopping on the brink.
- Breathe in deeply, pulling back the belly to encourage the Flame to rise into the base chakra. From there breathe in again with a deep but short breath and suck the Fire up the spine and into the sacral chakra.
- Stimulate and breathe the Fire up through all the chakras, feeling each one light up in turn until the crown is reached.
- When the Fire reaches the crown, breathe out long and slow, allowing the Fire to cascade back down through the body and the aura, irradiating every cell, until it reaches the base chakra once again and connects to the grounding root and the Earth Star chakra.
- Begin the process again. With practice it will be possible to raise the Fire seven times in a controlled flow that is then coiled into the centre of power that is the dantien ('The Cave of Min' above the sacral chakra just below the navel) to be stored until required.
- At this point, control is released and full orgasm takes place.
- Following this stage, the Fire is encouraged to rise above

the crown chakra into the Soul Star and Stellar Gateway chakras and from there cascade down the outer edges of the aura to link to the Earth Star and Gaia Gateway chakras beneath the feet.

Linking in the higher chakras both 'above' and 'below' in this way provides an anchoring and grounding for the spiritual force to flash down through the chakras above the head, uniting with the physical sexual force rising to meet it. Repeat the exercise at least three times more until raising the Flame becomes automatic. You think it, and it occurs.

- From this point on, full orgasm is raised and released up to seven times in one session, raising and flooding the ecstatic Power of Sekhem throughout the whole physical and subtle body systems to unite 'above' and 'below'.

Raising the Fire of Min

Using the power of your imagination and visualisation to activate and picture your inner male energies, the animus, raise the Power of Min as described in the next chapter. It will flow up your spine as a counterpoint to the Fire of Mut. Repeat three or seven times.

Raising the combined Flames

Once both Flames are mastered, use physical and imaginal working to raise both Flames simultaneously up your spine, rising from the sacrum (sacred bone) in harmony. Repeat three or seven times.

Fire of Mut raising crystals: Fire Opal, Garnet, Kundalini Quartz, Poppy Jasper, Red Zincite, Serpentine, Triplite, Black Basalt or Sandstone Shiva Lingam. *(Place at the feet or on the base chakra.)*

Fire of Mut controlling crystals: Anandalite, Brown flash Ethiopian Opal, Jet with Serpentine, Magnetite, Red Amethyst, Serpentine. *(Place above the head.)*

Once this union and raising is achieved, this stage of the alchemical process is complete.

Chapter 7

Raising the Fire of Min (the male Flame)

This is where the male initiate learns to master the Fire of Min preparatory to raising The Power of Sekhem and bending it to his will. As P.B.R. states, "The object of this exercise is to simultaneously raise the sacred Fire and gain control over the process." The object is orgasm without ejaculation. At no point must ejaculation take place until the raising has been fully mastered. It may take a certain amount of practice to achieve this seven times. Seven was the magical number of completion and perfection in ancient Egypt. The ultimate orgasm, it gave mastery over Set, the power of darkness. Use of a controlling crystal assists the process.

The Alchemy of Night Enchiridion

IV

Raising the Fire of Min

The Alchemy of Night Enchiridion

Raising the male Flame

As the Great God Min raised the Ben Ben on the primeval mound out of the waters of chaos by the act of his hand,[1] so shall the Adept by sau raise the sacred Fire in an Act of Will that transforms the mundane world.

Having bathed and purified the body with salt and incense, the Adept must first anoint the Great Central Suns[2] with Oil of Blue Lotus in a circular motion following the Great Sun God from east to west[3] and through the Gates of Night to greet the dawn and salute the rising God once more. Each Central Sun is then saluted in turn. The Adept stands with feet apart facing the Great God. Keeping the feet planted firmly on the Earth he listens to the heart beat within, to the Soul fluttering softly within the body. With each beat he rotates the hips first to the front, then to the right hand side, to the back and to the left hand side seven times. Without pause, he reverses the direction and rotates for seven more circles. Wait. Breathe.

* * *

The Gateway is opened.

* * *

The Adept seats himself during the morning hours, the time of maximum potency for the male. To raise the sacred Fire, he places the middle digit of the left hand on the perineum behind the scrotal sac and the first digit to the right of the testes with the third digit to the left side. He presses firmly to awaken the sleeping God and activate the Fire of Min.

The shaft of the henn is grasped with the right hand close

to its base and the Staff of Min drawn up to stand proud like the Ben Ben rising from the Mound of Creation. As the Great God brought the world into being so the hand of the Adept creates anew. The rocking motion of the hand begins to raise the sacred Fire towards the Head of Min. As the Fire rises, so does the hand until it is engaged under the Head of the God. The Adept pulls back the belly and breathes deeply into the scrotal sac, allowing the sacred Fire to flow into the Great Central Sun of Osiris.[2] Taking the Breath of Life deep into the Sun of Osiris,[3] he holds it there for as a long as possible. Keeping the buttocks and perineum firmly clenched, he allows the Fire to rise like a serpent up the spinal column opening the Secret Eye of the Belly. With each breath the Fire rises higher, twining through and lighting up each of the Great Central Suns. At no time in this stage of initiation must *Seti*[4] be spilt. His right hand must hold as still as the mouse scented by the falcon until the urge to void the Seti ceases. The Adept must begin again, pulling the generative force ever higher up the spine and through the Central Suns. So does the Will learn to overcome Desire. When the Fire reaches the heart it stimulates the seat of the Soul which entwines with the Fire of Min to stimulate the Secret Chambers of the Central Suns. With every breath and each movement of the hand, the Fire rises ever higher until it reaches the Gate of Min and the Great Cause of Light ignites above the head.

At the crown, as the Adept exhales long and slow, the Fire cascades down through the body, arms and hands and meets the Staff of Min Below. The Fire becomes a great circle uniting the Khat, material body, the Ba and the Great God. Cascading through the whole of the Adept's being, it animates the *Khu*, bringing the Great Body of Light closer to infuse the *ka* and the whole of the physical and spiritual being. So below, as above. The Neters are brought to the Earth and the Adept closer to the Heavens. The Adept may truly say: "I am become the God. I am become Divine."

Repeat until the Fire has been lit seven times. Once this is achieved, the Adept may use the Power of the Heart to master and direct the Fire to circle in and store it beneath the navel in the Cave of Min.[5]

* * *

Practice over the course of several weeks may be required before the sacred Fire can be lit seven times without Seti. This practice, when under the control of the Will, irradiates with orgasmic force the Secret Chambers of the Central Suns.[6] Once this occurs, Seti may take place – at the same time taking the attention up through the body as the orgasmic spasm progresses to unite heart and mind, body and soul with the divine force and facilitate control by the Higher Will over the process.

Once true mastery has been achieved, the orgasmic force will be raised purely by the power of Sekhem itself. It is seen in the Eye of the Mind and the force rises of its own volition and Will. The Adept has become the God incarnate, the embodiment of the God and is ready to be united with the Flames of Mut.

Commentary

The objective of this exercise is to simultaneously raise the sacred Fire and give the Adept control over the process. Strict discipline must be maintained to master the flow of Fire and link it to the subtle endocrine system and to the Soul. The ancient Prince was at pains to point out that spilling seed invalidates this stage of the proceedings. The urge to ejaculate must be mastered by the force of the Will. Orgasm without ejaculation being a powerful raiser of kundalini energy in this step of the initiation process. Later the seed may be spilled, particularly into a sacred vessel specially prepared to receive it – that is the fully initiated female Twinflame of the Adept. Or, as I have discovered, for the purpose of sanctification and activation of a magic mirror or other magical tool. But I cannot speak of this here.

If the Adept finds this process difficult, he may alter the breathing pattern to short and rapid 'pants'. A huffing and puffing that raises the Fire and holds it within each Central Sun as it passes through. This is not such a thorough orgasmic infiltration, but it may act as a step along the path of initiation. It may assist the Adept to know that the left side of the prostate gland is material, and the right side spiritual, emotional and mental and to visualise these two streams rising up the spine. The root chakra holds the balance. Stimulating all three points activates the Leydig gland that sits above the testes. This is the seat of kundalini power in the male and the key to opening the Central Sun of Creation.

Dr. P.B.R.

Addendum notes

The whole process is somewhat similar to the raising of the Kundalini Force as taught by the Eastern Philosophies and embodied within Theosophical teachings. It imbues the body with creative energy, lodging it in the intercellular structures of the bodies both material and spiritual. The process culminates in *en-lighten-ment*. The bliss of Divine Union.

1   Another example of the earlier recension of Egyptian creationism. The Fertility God Min rather than Ra here brings the world into being.
2   The Great Central Sun of Osiris is the base chakra in the Theosophical tradition.
3   Clockwise.
4   Seti is the action of ejaculating semen or impregnating a female partner.
5   Cave of Min: The dantien in Eastern Philosophy.
6   The endocrine system.

E.A.W.B.

Modern commentary

Male initiation

This is where the male initiate moves deep into the process of *The Alchemy of Night*, stirring the sexual force (the Fire of Min) into being and bringing it up the spine so that the act of self-pleasuring becomes mastery of spiritual unity with the divine. It is important that ejaculation does not take place until the practice has been mastered and the uniting of 'above' with 'below' is fully integrated. The Power of Sekhmet is then activated. The exercise should follow a period of abstinence and purification of the chakras.

Preparation

Prepare your space carefully. Bathe in warm water that has good-quality ylang ylang oil and Halite or Himalayan salt added. Put on a robe or fresh clothes. Burn appropriate candles and anoint yourself with good-quality ylang ylang oil if Oil of Blue Lotus is not available. The use of raising and controlling crystals and your grounding root ensures that the Flame will not rise in an uncontrolled fashion or shoot off at a tangent rather than smoothly rising up the spine. Ensure that you will not be disturbed as each step should lead seamlessly into the next.

Timing

The Prince identifies sunrise as the optimum time for a male to work this rite. P.B.R. suggests that any time in the evening or between three and eight o'clock in the morning would be appropriate. But see also the ultradian rest-phase cycle on page 12, which could identify the best time for you.

Step 1: Anointing the chakras

- Beginning with the base chakra and using a circular

movement in the direction that is right for you, with a fingertip rub a little Ylang Ylang or Blue Lotus oil into each chakra in turn. Breathe deeply into your belly as you do so, taking the fragrance deep within yourself. As you breathe out, feel the energy beginning to rise to the next chakra.

- Continue until all the chakras up to the crown have been activated.

Step 2: The activating movements

Playing a shamanic drum heart-rhythm assists with this stage.

- Stand with your feet apart, facing south.
- Pause for a moment and listen to the beat of your heart.
- With each beat, move your hips to the rhythm. First to the front, then out to the right-hand side, to the rear, and across to the left and then back to the resting position.
- Repeat seven times.
- Then reverse the direction.
- Standing quietly, breathe gently. Feel the gateway at the base of the spine opening and the Fire of Min waiting to rise.

Step 3: Raising the Sacred Flame

- Seat yourself in a quiet room or lie down if this is more comfortable.
- Ensure that your grounding root is in place.
- Place a raising crystal over your base chakra.
- Feel the chakras opening above your head and light pouring down into your crown and from there through all the chakras to your feet. Anchor it to your Earth Star.
- Place a Power of Sekhem controlling crystal over your head (a beanie hat holds it in place).
- Place the middle finger of your left hand on the perineum behind the scrotal sac. Press the first finger to the right of

the testes with the third finger to the left side. Press firmly to awaken the Fire of Min.

- Grasp the shaft of the penis with the right hand close to the base so that it stands erect.
- With a rocking movement, begin to pull the Fire upwards until the hand is engaged beneath the head of the penis.
- Breathe deeply into the scrotal sac, pulling it tight to encourage the Flame of Min to flow into the base chakra. Hold for as long as possible.
- Keeping the buttocks firmly clenched and the perineum drawn up, pull the Flame upwards. Rhythmically contracting the perineum in harmony with your breathing assists the process from hereon.
- At no point in the rite should semen be spilt. Cease movement and hold still until the possibility of ejaculation subsides but the Flame moves ever upward. Then begin again.
- Breathe in again with a deep but short breath and suck the Fire up the spine and into the sacral chakra. Clench and hold as you breathe out.
- Breathe the Fire up through all the chakras, feeling each one light up in turn until the crown is reached.
- When the Fire reaches the crown, breathe out long and slow, allowing the Fire to cascade back down through the body and the aura, irradiating every cell, until it reaches the base chakra once again and connects to the grounding root and the Earth Star chakra.
- Begin the process again. With practice it will be possible to raise the Fire seven times without ejaculation in a controlled flow that is then coiled into the centre of power that is the dantien ('The Cave of Min' above the sacral chakra just below the navel) to be stored until required.
- At that stage, full orgasm occurs and the Fire is encouraged to rise above the crown chakra into the Soul Star and Stellar Gateway chakras and from there cascade down the outer

aura to link to the Earth Star and Gaia Gateway chakras beneath the feet.

- The Power of Sekhem will be activated.

Linking in the higher chakras both 'above' and 'below' in this way provides an anchoring and grounding for the psycho-spiritual force that is the Power of Sekhem to flash through the chakras above the head, uniting with the physical sexual force. Repeat the exercise at least three times more until it becomes automatic. You *think* it, and it occurs.

Raising the Fire of Mut

Using the power of your imagination and visualisation to activate and picture your inner female energies, the anima, raise the Power of Mut as described in the last chapter. It will flow up your spine as a counterpoint to the Fire of Min. Repeat three or seven times.

Raising the combined Flames

Once both Flames are mastered, use physical and imaginal working to raise both Flames simultaneously up your spine, rising from the sacrum (sacred bone) in harmony. Repeat three or seven times.

Fire of Min raising crystals: Fire Opal, Garnet, Kundalini Quartz, Poppy Jasper, Red Zincite, Serpentine, Triplite, Black Basalt or Sandstone Shiva Lingam. *(Place at the feet or on the base chakra.)*

Fire of Min controlling crystals: Anandalite, Hematite, Jet with Serpentine, Magnetite, Moqui Marbles, Petrified Wood, Red Amethyst, Rutilated Quartz, Serpentine. *(Place above the head or over the base or sacral chakra.)*

Once this union and raising is achieved at will, this stage of the alchemical process is complete.

Chapter 8

Raising the twin flames in unison

Now comes the moment when, if working alongside a magical partner, the twin flames are raised in unison. A powerful test of mastery of the will, this is not the ultimate mystic marriage. But is an important preparatory stage along the way. Once again, it requires controlled orgasm without ejaculation. If working alone, use your imagination!

The Alchemy of Night Enchiridion

V

Raising Min and Mut in Unison

The Alchemy of Night Enchiridion

Raising the twin flames

Once the Fires of Min and Mut have been aroused in the individual Adepts, the moment comes when the two Spiritual Flames must be commingled in the Spiritual Bodies of the Beloved, the Priestess of the Heart and the Priest of the Soul who were promised to each other before birth. But the Adepts must be aware. This is not the Mystic Marriage they yearn for. This commingling is not one of physicality, it is of the Soul. A union of God and Goddess, of the Divine Ones. This is a preparatory stage and each must cleave to the other in Spirit only, not in body. There will be no *nedjemit ndjemu* ['love joys' or sexual pleasure] at this stage. A powerful test of Will, the mutual raising of the Flames without Seti is one of the last tests, perhaps the greatest of all the tests. The culmination of the training that has been undertaken for so long.

* * *

Having fasted all day, in the cool of an evening when the Light of Khonsu has risen to its full tide, the Adepts, having made their ablutions and offerings, stand together and disrobe. Each slowly anoints the Central Suns of the other with the Oil of Blue Lotus, feeling the sacred Fire rise within. Each in turn intones:

We are become the Divine, the Great God and the Great Goddess incarnate.

They lie down on their right sides, male behind female, Great Central Sun touching Central Sun. The arms of the male enfold the female and rest on her Seat of the Soul. The female's hands cover his. Not a muscle is moved as, breathing rhythmically and deeply in slow unison, they activate The Power of Sekhem to open the inner eye and raise the Fires of Mut and Min. Each feels both currents rising up the spine, reaching out to the other, intertwining, activating the Secret Chambers and bringing the flames to the Heart. Burning in the ecstasy of the Divine, the flames rise to the Great Light Above, cascading down to begin the cycle again. Breathing, holding, breathing, holding, breathing, pulling up the Fires until God and Goddess are engulfed and the powers are commingled and sealed into place. No seed must be spilled so that the orgasmic force vivifies every part of the being uniting all the soulbodies and embodying the Sakhu here on the Earth. The Great Orgasm of Creation is complete. The Souls are forever joined.

* * *

The Adepts must each make the sacred Inner Marriage with the Eternal One Within before moving on to the Mystic Marriage between man and woman that will commingle the two natures, physical and spiritual, and manifest the Divine on Earth.

Commentary

This is marriage on the inner spiritual planes as taught to my Adepts in the Brotherhood of Eulis. Once again the Prince is at pains to point out that, at this stage, no semen should be spilled. It is a union on the energetic planes. Union on the physical will come later. This is an activation and integration of chakric union that surpasses the material and lasts throughout eternity which must be devoutly wished for and undertaken with dedication and deep love.

It is my experience that marriages on the physical plane fail because partners suffer from magnetic and vital fluid exhaustion. The nervo-vital fluid links the body and spirit and soul to Aeth, an infinite reservoir. But only when the Alchemy of

Night practice is strictly followed. There is a need for electrical, magnetic, and chemical reciprocation. A blending of natures and of intensity and diffusion. The Wills must be united in a common purpose. Above all, the partners must adhere to the naturally waxing and waning cycles of sexual power, passion and interest. Never must the act be forced. If these precepts are respected, the sexual commingling of natures will be fully restorative.

Dr. P.B.R.

Modern commentary

Union on the inner planes

This is perhaps one of the most puzzling and challenging aspects of *The Alchemy of Night* process for a modern initiate. It is a sacred joining on the inner planes, bringing together physical and psycho-spiritual energies, and yet paradoxically appears to be an external event involving a.n.other, your magical physical twinflame. Trying to understand it with the head (intellectual mind) is counterproductive. Simply *allow*. Having said that, a fertile imagination is required as there is no physical stimulation to raise the Power of Sekhem other than the anointing of the chakras and the power of the mind.

The rite creates a non-physical, spiritual 'commingling of souls' for which Egyptian initiates prepared over a long period. It brings together the souls of two incarnated beings, the twinflames, and the spiritual forces of the masculine god and feminine goddess. The Prince regarded it as perhaps the greatest test of all. It requires a honed will and enormous self-control. If you are male, it calls for *non-seti*, 'orgasm without ejaculation'. If ejaculation does occur, then the process must be begun once more on the next full moon and the preceding rites practised again in the meantime until holding back ejaculation is mastered.

Timing

The evening of the full moon. The Scorpio full moon is ideal – i.e. during the zodiac sign of Taurus in late April to May. It could be repeated at midnight and at dawn if all three occurrences are to take place on the same full moon. Otherwise, space the rites out at full, new and full moon intervals – that is over the period of a month.

Preparation

The Prince called for a day of fasting to prepare for this rite. Drink plenty of fresh spring water or vegetable juices to cleanse the body and digestive system of any toxins that are released. In the evening, each partner should take a cleansing Halite, Himalayan or Epsom salt bath. Prepare your sacred space and offer up rose oil or incense to the gods. Ensure that your grounding roots are in place. The rite is worked naked in low light.

Anointing the chakras

- Standing facing inwards, each partner slowly anoints the chakras of the other in turn, applying Oil of Blue Lotus or high-quality Rose Oil. Consciously will the Power of Sekhem to rise up the spine as you do so, breathing it up and holding it there as each chakra is activated.
- Complete the anointing by passing the oil over the head and down to the floor to activate the highest crown chakras and connect them to the Gaia Gateway.
- Put the left hand on the partner's heart. Intone together, "We are become the Divine, the Great God and the Great Goddess incarnate."

The rite of commingling

- Ensure that your individual grounding roots are in place and the chakras over the head open.
- Lie on your right sides, male behind female with the chakras touching (the chakras extend to the back as well as the front of the body). The arms of the male enfold the female and rest on her heart. The female's hands cover his.
- Feel divine light pouring down through the crown chakras, activating the Power of Sekhem that lies at the base of the sacrum (sacred bone).

- Not a muscle is moved other than rhythmic contraction of the perineum and vagina, as, breathing rhythmically and deeply in slow unison, the Power of Sekhem is pulled up through each chakra in turn to open the Third (inner) Eye and raise the Fires of Mut and Min in tandem with the Power of Sekhem. Each partner feels the twin fires of the physical sexual force rising up the spine entwined with the psycho-spiritual Power of Sekhem. The flames reach out to meet the complementary Fire in the partner, intertwining, activating the chakras and bringing the flames and the Power into the heart and to the crown.

- Breathe, hold, breathe, hold, breathe, hold again, pulling up the Fires and Power until you are both engulfed in a divine conflagration. This is best described as 'Burning in the ecstasy of the Divine'. Rise up out of your bodies and into communion with the divine through the higher crown chakras. The souls and the divine powers are commingled and sealed into place. It is a sacred union with the 'Great Light Above'.

- Then, cascade the Power of Sekhem down around the edges of the subtle bodies to the Gaia Gateway to begin the cycle again.

- The Prince warns that "no seed must be spilled so that the orgasmic force vivifies every part of the being uniting all the soul-bodies and embodying the *Sakhu* (highest soulbody) here on the Earth."

- The Prince also states, "The Great Orgasm of Creation is complete. The Souls are forever joined." For the modern day, it might be more appropriate to make the joining for as long as the relationship shall last – remember to perform a 'spiritual divorce (see Appendix III)' should the relationship end prematurely.

Repeat the rite at least three times until it becomes automatic.

115

When you have mastered it, you can picture it in your imagination, will it, and the commingling occurs without effort.

Where possible, the rite should end there, without physical orgasm, as this will make the cosmic orgasm that much more powerful when it finally occurs. But if you simply cannot wait, ejaculation and full orgiastic ecstasy should occur simultaneously for both partners.

There now remains one further stage before the mystic marriage is made.

Chapter 9

Entering into marriage with the eternal one

The stage has now been reached where the initiate makes a personal sacred marriage with the inner divine spark or 'the Eternal One' as the Prince expresses it. This is a rite to work alone, having made the appropriate preparations. It is the final rite before the mystic marriage with a twinflame takes place. The rite utilises the power of the imagination and visualisation, which has by now been honed into a finely woven magical tool.

The Alchemy of Night Enchiridion

VI

Entering into Marriage with the Eternal One

The Alchemy of Night Enchiridion

Sacred marriage with the divine

Seated in sacred space, the Adept takes ten slow, deep breaths withdrawing into the inner silence. The Adept breathes gently, establishing an even rhythm. The eyelids grow heavy and lie softly on the face. The Adept steps out of the *Khat*, the physical body, into the Soulbody, the *Ka*, which stands up. The external world falls away to reveal the inner planes.

In the mind's eye the Adept stands in the entrance to a vast temple. Before the Adept there are tall walls with their high, ornate wooden gates covered in beaten gold. These are the gates to the inner courtyard. Slowly these gates open inwards. A temple guardian beckons the Adept in.

The guardian conducts the Adept to a chamber in the inner courtyard. In this chamber a bathing place has been prepared. Temple *eibatas* bathe, dry and perfume the Adept with Oil of Blue Lotus and dress the Adept in new robes to prepare for the marriage. When the Adept is ready, the guardian takes the Adept to the offering chamber. The Adept makes an offering to ensure a successful inner marriage. Whatever is most appropriate is offered with reverence on the altar and the Adept turns to leave.

The guardian conducts the Adept into the nuptive chamber to await the Divine Partner in this inner marriage. Food is prepared, drink awaits. Behind thin, gauzy curtains the marriage bed beckons. When the guardian withdraws, the divine partner comes to the Adept. The sacred prostration is made and the presence of the Above awaited. When the divine being appears, the Adept humbly offers their own being to Above.

The Divine One raises up the Adept and leads them to the bridal bed. The Divine One whispers into the ear of the Adept the Secret Name that conveys dominion over the divine force. The Adept swears never to reveal this name: the Secret Name of

God is sacrosanct. This name gives all power and dominion to the Adept, with this name the Adept may control the forces of Creation and command the Divinities themselves.

This union is a total merging, a marriage on all levels, a pullulating ecstasy with the divine. Allowing the inner partner, the Divine Form Within, to come into the Great Central Sun of the Heart, to merge, to join with Soul, the Adept lets the Divine One do as they will to instil the divine essence within. But if the Adept is a male, Seti must not occur.

* * *

When it is time to leave the bridal chamber, the temple guardian comes to conduct the Adept and the Inner Divine Partner back to the doors leading into the outside world. Walk with the guardian across the courtyard. Take off the sacred robe and put on that which is suitable for the outer world.

The Adept steps out of the gates knowing wholeness within. The masculine and feminine energies have been integrated, God and Goddess, Above and Below, the Human and the Divine, the Soul with the Great Ones.

Standing outside the temple, the Adept is surrounded and protected by the Light of the Great Sun-God. The Ka walks to the physical body, the two integrating once more. The Adept breathes more deeply and stamps the right foot on the ground three times to close the inner door. At this juncture the female Adept is to be awarded the *Menat*[1] amulet with its combined male and female organs of generation that signifies freedom from the erotic cravings of lesser beings and canalisation of desire into ability to rise above the limitations of the earthly being. The male Adept is awarded the *Sem*[2] amulet with its risen phallus that signifies desire tamed into pure power. The holder of the *Menat* and the *Sem* rises Above into the pullulating raptures of male-female union and into the vitality of the Power of New Life.

Commentary: Affectional Alchemy

The first stage of the mystic marriage conflates the complementary Divine Energy with the Human Soul through the power of the imagination which, to the ancients, was as powerful a force as actual union, if not more so. Indeed imagination was the vivifying force that brought the material and the sacred into manifestation. In ancient times both rituals would have taken place in a small temple within the main complex but this can be replicated within the space in which group practice takes place or within the Adept's own home. Prepare your sacred space carefully with incense to cleanse and sanctify it. The first ritual takes place within the mind's eye but the more fully the Adept can experience the sensations, sounds and smells, the deeper will be the integration of the human Soul with the divine. If working alone, the Adept must visualise the guardian. If working in a group, a group member can lead the Adept to the marriage bed and other group members assist with the ritual bathing and robing.

In preparation, the Adept is bathed in water laden with salt, dried, purified with incense, each of the Seven Great Central Suns is anointed with Oil of Blue Lotus and the Adept robed in the marriage gown. This preparation may be physically carried out prior to the ritual and again in the mind's eye during the ritual. In the ancient ritual stance the Adept sits with back straight and feet firmly on the floor. In modern day rituals the Adept may prefer a marriage bed. Make for yourself a bridal bed with silken sheets, veiled and strewn with rose petals on which to lie.

Dr. P.B.R.

Addendum notes

1   The *Menat* amulet was of glazed ware or carved stone shaped into a gourd-like container suspended on a necklace with a counterbalancing crescent.

2   The *Sem* amulet was a phallus enclosed within the headdress

of Min and counterbalanced by the fiery sun. Placed on the back of the neck the amulets activated a chakra within the head of the Adept, lifting sexuality to a higher level of functioning. The *Menat* was the means through which Goddess power was transmitted and the *Sem* that of the God. It was believed to move desire to an altogether higher plane of ecstasy through mastery of the forces of earthly lust, the union of souls and rising up beyond the stars. It was in direct contrast to the Sema amulet, used in ancient Egyptian love spells, which bound two souls in earthly desire and the rapturous satisfaction of lust at the lower level of the physical body only with no soul union taking place. When the more physically powerful on the physical plane *Sema* amulet was brought into play, the desired female would be irresistibly drawn to yield all in self-surrender to the powers of lust that would bind the souls to earthly desire across the centuries.

E.A.W.B.

Modern commentary

Mystic marriage with the Highest Self

This is where the initiate makes a personal powerful inner soul bond with the *Sakhu* or Highest Self. Yin and yang, masculine and feminine, are indissolubly united with the divine spark within. After the usual preparations as to creating safe space, bathing, anointing the chakras and so on, the rite commences. It is intended to be worked alone, in silence and undisturbed. However, if you are working with your twinflame in unison, you may prefer your twinflame to guide you through the steps of the ritual, a deeply intimate process.

If necessary, record the visualisation, leaving appropriate pauses, and play it as you work the rite.

The inner marriage rite

- Seated in sacred space, take ten slow, deep breaths withdrawing into the inner silence. Breathe gently, establishing an even rhythm. Your eyelids grow heavy and lie softly on your face.
- Step out of your physical body, move into the Soul-body, the *Ka*, which stands up. The external world falls away to reveal the inner planes.
- In your mind's eye, you stand at the entrance to a vast temple. Tall walls are broken by high, ornate wooden gates covered in beaten gold.
- Slowly these gates open inwards. A temple guardian beckons you into the inner courtyard.
- The guardian conducts you to a side chamber. In this chamber a bathing place has been prepared. Temple assistants bathe, dry and perfume you with Oil of Blue Lotus. They dress you in fresh robes to prepare for the

marriage.

- When you are ready, the guardian takes you to the offering chamber to make an offering to ensure a successful inner marriage. Whatever is most appropriate is offered with reverence on the altar and then you turn to leave.

- You are conducted into the marriage chamber to await the Divine Partner. Food is offered, drink awaits. Behind thin, gauzy curtains the marriage bed beckons.

- As the guardian leaves, the divine partner steps towards you. You lower yourself to the floor in a sacred prostration, honouring the divine spark within your own Self. You humbly offer your own being to the Light Above.

- The divine partner raises you up and leads you through the curtains to the bridal bed.

- Standing close together, the divine partner whispers into your ear the *Ren*, the secret name that gives you power to direct the divine force. You swear on your very life never to reveal this name: the Secret Name is sacrosanct. With this name you may control the forces of Creation and command the Divinities themselves.

- The divine partner takes you to bed. This union is a total merging, a marriage on all levels, "pullulating ecstasy with the divine". Encourage the divine partner to do as they will to bring you to the brink of orgasm to instil the divine essence within. But, if you are a male, physical ejaculation must not occur. You must hold back in the way that you have learned, allowing the sensation to cascade through your whole being.

- Open your heart, encouraging the partner, the 'Divine Spark Within', to reach into your heart chakra, to merge, to join with your soul.

- You become as one. The divine partner now resides within your Heart Seed chakra.

- When it is time to leave the bridal chamber, the temple

guardian comes to conduct you back to the doors leading into the outside world. Walk with the guardian across the courtyard. Take off the sacred robe and put on that which is suitable for the outer world.

- Step through the gates knowing wholeness within. The masculine and feminine energies have been integrated, God and Goddess, Above and Below, the Human and the Divine, the Soul with the Great Ones.
- Standing outside the temple, you are surrounded and protected by Light. Your Ka walks to your physical body and settles in, the two integrating once more.
- Breathe more deeply, becoming aware of your surroundings. Move your fingers and toes. Stretch out your arms. Stamp the right foot on the ground three times to close the inner door.
- Ensure that your grounding cord is in place.

You now have infused within you the vitality of the Power of New Life. The mystic marriage with your own Highest Self is complete. You are entitled to wear a Menat or Sem amulet as a symbol of initiation.

Chapter 10

Commencing the Mystic Marriage

Finally, the initiates reach the stage whereby together they celebrate the mystic marriage and attain cosmic orgasm. In ancient times, this was a ritual awakening attended by priests, priestesses and attendants after long preparation. The end of the Prince's papyrus was missing and, therefore, the final part of the rite lost. It has been reconstructed with the assistance of P.B.R. in the Codas that follow.

The Alchemy of Night Enchiridion

VII

The Mystic Marriage

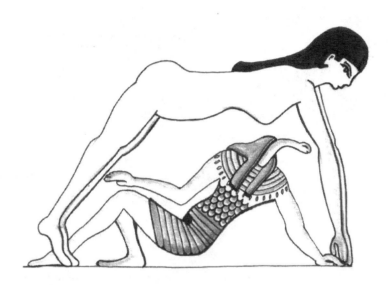

The Alchemy of Night Enchiridion

Mystic marriage between two souls

The preparation chamber of the male Adept is lit by lamps of gleaming basalt burning the purest oil. A lighted censor of cinnamon, cloves and frankincense purifies the air. The priests chant to the beat of a drum as the evening light dies. The senior priest intones:

"It is the perilous moment when time takes a breath, pauses, and stands still. At any moment the Great Sun God will leave the world of the living and enter the world of the dead, journeying on the Boat of the Sun through the darkest passages of night to fight his enemies."

The Adept is exhorted: "Be strong, be brave, be truthful, be new. You have the God Within. The Great God Min waits to be born anew."

The Adept replies: "My ka has prevailed over my enemies, my ba knows the ways that lead to the gate that conceals the Sight."

The Adept's head is shorn of its plaited sidelock, the symbols of initiation stand out clearly. Every inch of his body carefully shaved, not a single hair must defile the presence of the Gods. He is anointed with the sacred oils and his henn wrapped in a loincloth of finest linen, a garland of Blue Lotus placed around his neck. And the Sem amulet is placed at the Doorway to Infinity.[1] A cup of potent lotus wine laced with mandrake root is handed to him. He drinks deep. He has become the God.

* * *

The preparation chamber of the female Adept is lit by pots of finest alabaster. The censor burns cinnamon, ambergris and Blue Lotus flower to purify the air.

Priestesses chant in the evening light: "It is the precious moment when day turns to night. We are with you, child, be brave, be bold, be powerful. You have the Goddess Within. The Lady Mut waits to be born anew."[2]

The high priestess asks: "Are you wowaei, one who has not been opened by childbirth?"[3]

The initiate replies: "Never have I been opened by child. I am kheroti. My ka prevailed over my enemies, my ba knows the ways that lead to the gate that conceals the Sight."

The Adept's body is carefully shaved and her body rubbed with the sweet-smelling oils, her lips and kabits are tipped with carmine, and a transparent robe of finest blue linen is tied beneath her firm young breasts, a garland of Blue Lotus placed around her neck with the Menat amulet at the Gate of Infinity. The nine concentric rings of an initiate of Mut stand out clearly on her upper arm. A cup of potent lotus wine laced with mandrake root is handed to her. She drinks deep. She has become the Goddess.

* * *

From the Temple of Mut the sistrums thrum, high female voices rise and fall in joyful harmony as the procession begins. From the Temple of Min the drums throb, insistent and deep. Male voices chant long and slow. The processions weave snake-like paths across the darkening night towards the sanctuary of She Who Is Powerful.

"Who comes through the night to risk the Foes of Min?"

"An Adept who has fulfilled the nine initiations and seeks to make the final joining with his beloved, his chosen one. For this I was born."

"Who comes through the night to disturb the peace of My Lady?"

"An Adept who has passed the nine initiations and seeks to make the final joining with her beloved, her chosen one. For this

I was born."

"Are you aware of the grave sanctity of this act? That with this mystic marriage comes a joining for all time? That you will never be free from each other again no matter where your Souls may wander?"

"We are and we seek to claim our birthright. For this we were born."

"Enter the sacred portals, make your offering and complete your initiation."

The door to the sanctuary opens and hand in hand the two adepts move forward. Placing their offering of beer, bread and spices on the altar before them they move ever deeper into the sanctuary until they stand before The Lady. Picking up the cups of potent beer from her feet they lace their arms like serpents in the night, each offering the cup to The Lady and then to the other to drink deep. Solemnly they face each other taking the garlands from each other's neck. They turn to the towering statue, raising their hands above their heads before prostrating themselves full length on the ground for a long heartbeat of silence...

Standing once more the Adept takes...

... he touches it to the secret...

... God's plenty...

... to the... Eye of the Belly...

... And plac... middle digit... the Vein of Love...

[Commentator's note: The papyrus is wholly torn away at this point and there is no further text.]

Commentary

In ancient times the Mystic Marriage with the Great Divine would be solemnised between a young priest and priestess who had already made their own Marriage with the Eternal One within their own being and had united their souls on the spiritual plane, and who, therefore, could embody the God and the Goddess and bring them into physical and Soul union. This was the final stage of alchemical sexual initiation: the commingling of the divine so that the divine principle became embodied and manifested on the earth and in the Other World. Unfortunately the papyrus is blotched and torn at this point and the remainder of the ritual is lost.

Dr. P.B.R.

Addendum notes

It is exceedingly unfortunate that the remainder of this irreplaceable Work is lost. I am of the opinion that it went far beyond what Dr P.B.R. taught his initiates. That he clearly had glimpses of the expanded possibilities is obvious from his other writings but not delineated here.

1 The doorway to infinity is the hollow at the base of the skull above the spinal column. It would appear that this was the key to yet another chakra, the alta major, although the Prince does not further delineate the function of this chakra in the fragments that remain.

2 The evening of the new moon.

3 One who has not been opened in childbirth is virgin, set aside, sacred in herself. It would appear that the ancient Egyptians regarded virginity as having been discarded with pregnancy rather than with initial penetration.

E.A.W.B.

Modern commentary

Mystic marriage with the Beloved Twinflame

As this rite will most probably not take place in a formal temple, you will need to create your own, specially consecrated ritual space. Ideally the initiates should prepare themselves in separate rooms and then process to the bedroom, which has been thoroughly cleansed with space-clearing crystal essence (see page 160). Place new, clean linen on the bed – the Prince suggests sensuous silk – and wear fresh robes. Burn Oil of Frankincense in an oil burner if Blue Lotus oil is not available. Light beeswax candles. Place a statue of the goddess Sekhmet in a prominent position and the offering nearby. Position appropriate crystals under the head, middle, and foot of the bed. In ancient Egypt, the body was shorn of all hair. In the modern world this may be taken as far as you wish. A haircut and freshly washed hair rather than shaving the head is perfectly acceptable.

If you have a trusted friend who is used to ritual or sacred working and who could take on the role of priest or priestess, ask them to read the invocation and conduct the initial questioning for you. If not, read them together in unison or as question and answer between you as appropriate.

If you are a same sex couple, adapt the questions and rite as appropriate.

You will need:

A suitable 'magical brew'. Ginger, cardamom, cinnamon and clove herbal tea is an easily-obtained replacement for the magical brew drunk by the ancient Egyptians. Prepare it in advance and keep it in a flask.

A statue or picture of the Goddess Sekhmet.

An offering of bread, spices and beer.

Beer or other appropriate drink.

Initiation by Stephen Halpern, a chant recorded in the Great Pyramid, or his *Ancient Echoes*, is an excellent accompaniment to this ritual. It sets the mood perfectly and instantly takes you into a state of heightened awareness.

Timing: Sunset on a dark of the moon evening, i.e. just before new moon. Libra (October) or Pisces (March) would be a perfect time.

The joining rite

- Unless the commencement of the ritual is being conducted by someone taking the role of priest or priestess, join hands and chant the invocation together. If you have a conductor, he or she will say the invocation: "*It is the perilous moment when time takes a breath, pauses, and stands still. At any moment the Great Sun God will leave the world of the living and enter the world of the dead, journeying on the Boat of the Sun through the darkest passages of night to fight his enemies.*"
- The partners state in unison: "*We are strong, brave, truthful and new. We have the God and Goddess within. The Great God Min and the Goddess Mut wait to be born anew.*"
- The male (first) partner states: "*My ka has prevailed over my enemies. My ba knows the ways that lead to the gate that conceals the Sight.*"
- The conductor or the partner pours a cup of potent herbal tea and hands it across. Inhaling deeply, it is drunk slowly.
- The conductor, or the male (first) partner, asks the female (second) partner: "*Are you pure of mind and body?*"
- The female (second) partner replies: "*I am kheroti. My ka prevailed over my enemies, my ba knows the ways that lead to the gate that conceals the Sight.*"

- The conductor or the partner pours a cup of potent herbal tea and hands it over. Inhaling deeply, it is drunk slowly.
- The conductor, or the female partner, asks: "*Who comes through the night to risk the Foes of Min?*"
- The answer is given: "*A seeker who has fulfilled the initiations and seeks to make the final joining with his beloved, his chosen one. For this I was born.*"
- The conductor, or the male initiate, asks: "*Who comes through the night to disturb the peace of My Lady?*"
- The reply is given: "*A seeker who has passed the initiations and seeks to make the final joining with her beloved, her chosen one. For this I was born.*"
- The conductor, or the two partners in unison, asks: "*Are you aware of the grave sanctity of this act? That with this mystic marriage comes a joining for all time no matter where your Souls may wander?*" [If you prefer, change the wording to: "*This mystic marriage creates a soul union for as long as you both shall live together.*"]
- The reply is given: "*We are and we seek to claim our birthright. For this we were born.*"
- "*Enter the sacred portals, make your offering and complete your initiation.*"
- The conductor, if there is one, opens the door to the inner chamber and then withdraws.
- Hand in hand the partners move forward. Placing their offering of beer, bread and spices before The Lady.
- Picking up the cups of potent beer from her feet they lace their arms like serpents in the night, each offering the cup to The Lady and then to the other to drink deep. Solemnly they face each other raising their hands above their heads for a long heartbeat of silence.
- They touch their joined hands to the crown of the goddess and to that of each other.
- They move down the chakras, touching each in turn until

the base chakras are reached and the Power of Sekhem stirs.

The rite continues by opening the Alta Major chakra before moving to the bed to complete the mystic marriage and reach a mind-blowing cosmic orgasm. (See The First Coda, Chapter 11.)

Crystals for creating above and below unity: Celtic Quartz, Gaia's Blood and Milky Way Flint, K2, Lapis Lace Onyx, Lapis Lazuli, Purple Labradorite, Shiva Lingam.

Crystals to prolong sexual pleasure: Hematite, Poppy Jasper, Red Jasper.

Crystals to ground The Power of Sekhem into physical body and physical body to the planet: Ajoite or Ajo Quartz, Amphibole, Auralite 23, Azeztulite, Blue Aragonite, Boji Stones, Brown Triplite, Bustamite, Celtic Quartz, Elestial Quartz, Empowerite, Flint, Healer's Gold, Hematite, Herkimer Diamond, Lemurian Jade, Lemurian Seed, Libyan Gold Tektite, Merlinite, Mohawkite, Novaculite, Nunderite, Peanut Wood, Petrified Wood, Poppy Jasper, Preseli Bluestone, Purpurite, Quantum Quattro, Red Amethyst, Rutile with Hematite, Sedona Stone, Smoky Elestial Quartz, Smoky Herkimer, Smoky Quartz, Sodalite, Steatite, Stromatolite.

Crystals to raise The Power of Sekhem from the crown chakra to higher crown chakras: Amethyst, Amethyst with Hematite, Anandalite, Auralite 23, Brandenberg Amethyst, Celtic Quartz, Kundalini Quartz, Red Amethyst, Serpentine, Sugilite (Luvulite), Triplite, Vera Cruz Amethyst.

Chapter 11

Completing the mystic marriage and attaining cosmic orgasm

The remainder of the practice was reconstructed with the assistance of Dr P.R.B. Finally, ejaculation takes place and cosmic orgasm is achieved as the souls reunify with the whole of creation. Prior to this ultimate joining, a further chakra, the Alta Major, is opened and connected to the whole chakric system and the subtle bodies to create the receptive 'Golden Crown Diamond'. The whole system is then attached to a cosmic anchor point so that the souls will always find their way home.

The First Coda

Transcending self

The Alta Major: the seat of consciousness

The Alta Major

Location: Inside the skull and rising from the junction of the base of the skull and spine towards the third eye and the crown.

The Alta Major chakra is a major factor in accelerating and expanding consciousness. An anchor for the multidimensional lightbody (the *akhar*), reputedly it has been imprinted with 'divine codes' that, when activated, allow cosmic evolution to fully manifest on earth. The chakra creates a complex, Merkaba shape within the skull. It stretches from the base of the skull to the crown, connecting the past life chakras, hippocampus, hypothalamus, pineal and pituitary glands with the third eye, soma and higher crown chakras.[17]

The pineal gland works in conjunction with the subtle energy structure of the Alta Major. Along with the hypothalamus, it is the body's light meter and body clock regulator. In addition, the pineal contains crystalline 'brain sand', hydroxyapatite (found in Apatite, Fluorapatite and other crystals), which holds crystalline information. This metaphysical gland acts as a multidimensional energy structure into which higher vibrational energies anchor. It has been postulated that the pineal secretes DMT, the so-called 'spirit molecule'. A natural psychedelic, DMT is involved in out-of-body, near-death and other exceptional human experiences that take the soul into multidimensions and expanded vision.

The Alta Major chakra governs the behavioural, autonomic, and endocrine functions that keep the physical and subtle bodies in harmony with external factors including multidimensional consciousness. It facilitates becoming one with All That Is – one of the products of the Power of Sekhem activation. A well-balanced Alta Major vastly improves well-being, expanding consciousness and opening the Golden Crown Diamond of heart, mind, body, spirit and soul.

If at any time during the activating exercise you feel lightheaded, nauseous or dizzy, take your attention down to the grounding stone at your feet. Breathe deeply into the stone until the feeling stabilises. It is an excellent indication that the Alta Major is being recalibrated to accept expanded consciousness, which is then integrated into the entire chakra system. If the sensation becomes too intense, remove the Alta Major crystal, reground yourself and repeat the exercise later as the chakra may need to be activated in stages.

Activating the Alta Major

- Place a grounding stone such as Flint, Hematite or Smoky Quartz at your feet and check that your grounding root is in place.
- Use an Anandalite™ (Aurora Quartz), Blue Moonstone, Preseli Bluestone, Blue Kyanite or other Alta Major chakra crystal to activate the chakra. Place in the hollow at the base of the back of the skull. If necessary, place Preseli Bluestone, Rhomboid Selenite or Flint on the third eye to provide balance.
- Feel the Merkaba within your skull light up to connect up all the systems within your head and above your crown to the higher vibration chakras.
- Then picture the energy of the Alta Major reaching down to connect into your heart chakra, anchoring the energy there, and upwards to the higher crown chakras to connect mind, soul and spirit in the Golden Crown Diamond and anchor the lightbody.
- Return your awareness to the room and ensure your grounding root is in place. Stand up slowly.

Alta Major crystals: Anandalite, Angel's Wing Calcite, Apatite, Auralite 23, Azeztulite, Black Moonstone, Blue Kyanite, Blue Moonstone, Brandenberg Amethyst, Crystal Cap Amethyst, Diaspore (Zultanite), Eye of the Storm (Judy's Jasper), Fire and Ice Quartz, Golden Healer, Golden Herkimer Diamond, Green Ridge Quartz, Kyanite, Petalite, Phenacite, Preseli Bluestone.

Creating a cosmic anchor

A cosmic anchor complements the grounding cord, otherwise known as the shamanic anchor. The shamanic anchor holds you gently in incarnation and keeps your physical body connected to that of the planet. The cosmic anchor links your soul to the celestial realms so that, when you journey out of your physical body or enter a state of transcendental awareness, you will always find your way home – particularly from the multidimensions of consciousness and the multiverses beyond the one we currently inhabit. The tip of the centaur's arrow in the constellation of Sagittarius points at the galactic centre. It makes a useful 'hitching post' for the cosmic anchor. (See also The Third Coda.)

Creating a cosmic anchor

- Ensure that your grounding cord is in place.
- Place your hands over your navel and consciously move your attention up the spine, visualising a narrow tube that connects your grounding cord, which has now become a shamanic anchor, to the top of your head.
- From the crown chakra, send out another cord. This one goes to the sun, picking up its energy, and then it goes out through space to the constellation of Sagittarius. Here you hook your anchor on to the centaur's bow.
- Bring that cosmic anchor down to join your shamanic anchor at the point just under your navel that is the dantien, your personal power store.
- Remind yourself that, when taking a remote journey into interstellar space or multidimensional consciousness, you will return via the cosmic anchor.
- Bring your awareness back to your body and feel how your body is suspended by your cosmic anchor from the crown chakra to the centre of the galaxy, and by your shamanic anchor to the centre of the earth, joining at the dantien. Know that these anchors will always ensure you to return to your body no matter where you may journey.

Cosmic anchor crystals: Anandalite, Azeztulite, Blue Kyanite, Blue Moonstone, Brandenberg, Celestobarite, Celtic Quartz,

Fulgarite, Goethite, Lemurian Jade, Milky Way Flint, Prasiolite, Preseli Bluestone, Rutilated Quartz, Specular Hematite, Smoky Rose Quartz, White or Blue Flint.

The final stage: The mystic marriage

Finally the mystic marriage is completed, following on from the previous chapter having made the usual preparations, bathing and anointing the chakras and completing the invocation and offering. This part of the rite is conducted without clothing.

Completing the mystic marriage

- The female (second) partner sits on the partner's lap, facing him, with her legs around him. Where possible he should sit with legs folded in the lotus posture as this brings the chakras into close contact and opens the Power of Sekhem channel. If this is not possible, sit in as close an approximation as possible, leaning against a chairback or bedhead for support if necessary.
- Ensure that the grounding cords are in place.
- Maintain eye contact throughout.
- After appropriate foreplay, insert the penis into the vagina (or bring the sexual organs as close together as possible). No movement takes place other than a rhythmical contraction of the vagina and/or perineum and scrotum to raise the joint Power of Sekhem flames.
- When ejaculation is near, a male partner lays a hand on his partner's heart to still the contractions. A female partner lays a hand on her partner's heart if orgasm is close.
- The process begins again until joint orgasm without ejaculation occurs.
- On this first rise, the Power of Sekhem is taken out of the top of each head, up through the Soul Star where it is linked down the outer edges of the aura to the Earth Star, passing around the combined subtle bodies.
- On the second rise, it is raised to the Stellar Gateway

where it is joined to the Gaia Gateway.

- On the third rise, orgasm without ejaculation again takes place so that the Alta Major chakra is activated and integrated.

- The two souls combine to transcend the small self. The *kas* moving out of the physical bodies, into the lightbody, expanding beyond the chakras and auric bodies into multidimensional, divine consciousness. Moving beyond duality into total integrated consciousness (non-duality).

- Finally, ejaculation takes place and cosmic orgasm is experienced as the souls reunify with the whole of creation and higher vibrational energy floods through every level of being.

- Feel the shamanic grounding cords and the cosmic anchors holding you suspended between 'above' and 'below'. Weightless, timeless, limitless.

- At this point, should you choose to do so, you could journey anywhere and everywhere, into the highest possible reaches of the created and non-created universes. Ensure that your partner is aware and willing to participate in such a journey, or to hold the space for you to do so.

- If so, arrange a 'call-back' signal. A pull on the heart string connection between you that reminds you 'time to return'.

- When the time is right, settle gently back into your *khat,* your physical body, which will still be tingling with the reverberations of the cosmic orgasm. Draw that energy through every part of your being, consciously infusing each chakra, the intercellular spaces and vital bodies with the Power of Sekhem.

- After an appropriate pause and resting in quiet, timeless space, disentangle from your partner and lie down to sleep. Sleep curled around each other, chakra to chakra, to maintain the spiritual energetic contact for as long as possible.

- On awakening and again the next evening, repeat the cosmic orgasm if you wish to fulfil the promise of 'the rule of three'. Do so slowly, sensually, luxuriantly, revelling in each moment. Do not rush towards the finish. You have all the time in – and out – of the worlds.
- Before you return to the everyday world, close down each of the chakras in turn and ensure that your individual grounding root is in place and firmly anchored to the centre of the planet.

Note 1: If the rite is worked between same sex partners, the sex organs should touch as closely as possible and each raises the inner Flame in unison, signalling to the partner with hand on heart when a pause is required.

Note 2: If it is desired to conceive a physical divine child, ejaculation takes place on the third rise when the souls have been joined, the Alta Major activated and multidimensional, divine consciousness is reached. The resulting child will have very special metaphysical powers.

Chapter 12

Harnessing the magic of creation

By this stage you will be totally focused during your sexual conjugations, alone or with a partner; absolutely present in the moment, subsumed by the embodied transcendental divine energies. There is an unexpected bonus to prolonged arousal. The blissed-out on-the-brink orgasmic state is a potent one. Having built up your magical muscles as it were, you'll be ready to direct the primal force of The Power of Sekhem with a honed will and focused imagination, uniting it with the raw power of the earth and the universe, to open the magic of creation. Anything is possible. Creating in this way takes the manifestation process to a whole other level.

The Second Coda

Cosmic Manifestation

Cosmic creation

A most welcome by-product of the magic of *The Alchemy of Night* is the ability to bring into manifestation anything that you visualise or imagine. This includes healing and abundant well-being. The secret is to formulate your intention before commencement of the sexual act (alone or as a couple). Hold the intention strongly focused in your mind's eye until completion. Then let it go as the orgasmic feelings subside. Let the intention flow out into the ethers and leave the cosmos to do its work. This manifestation process works equally well as a solo act or in tandem with a partner – so long as a mutually agreeable intention is formulated in advance.

Preparation

Formulate your intention. Keep it simple and keep it ethical. An intention to take over the world – or another person – is unlikely to succeed. The intention to find more abundance in your life, to expand your spiritual awareness, or that healing and greater well-being will manifest will most likely be successful (if it's not, you might need to explore and reframe any old soul contracts or vows that are holding you back, see Appendix V, page 176). Be specific and be singular, work on one intention per session and wait until that is fulfilled before putting out another intention. You could choose a picture or a symbol that epitomises the intention – the subconscious and supraconscious minds work particularly well with symbols and images.

The Manifestation Rite

- Ensure that the grounding cord(s) is in place.
- Focus single-mindedly on your intention. Feel it with every part of your being. State your intention out loud, in

unison if you are working with a partner.

- Raise the Flames of Min and Mut through the chakras up to the crown and then bring The Power of Sekhmet up to your Alta Major chakra.
- Remain on the brink of orgasm for as long as possible. Build up the sexual energy slowly and powerfully. Stop, hold and breathe as necessary until your whole body is suffused with potent sexual force. Feel it flowing through and between every cell in your being. Your sexual organs, nipples, fingertips and toes will be zinging. Your spine will be on fire and your head about to explode.
- Bring your intention, or its symbol or image, to mind again and hold it there as you...
- Open the higher crown chakras and connect them to the Earth Star and Stellar Gateway.
- Draw energy up from the centre of the earth through the Gaia Gateway and connect it to the Stellar Gateway.
- Draw energy from the cosmos down through the Stellar Gateway and connect it to the Gaia Gateway.
- Feel the two forces mingling and joining in the dantien below your navel, and your Alta Major moving to a higher level of functioning.
- Finally, allow yourself to reach full orgasm. Pull the energy up from your dantien (below your navel) and let it flow out from the Alta Major. As you do so, shout aloud your intention to the universe.
- Float weightlessly, at one with creation.
- When your body has quietened again, withdraw your attention, reconnect your grounding cord, and leave the cosmos to do its work.

There is now no limit to where power of *The Alchemy of Night* may take you. Use it wisely and well.

Chapter 13

The Transcendental Flame

From the beginning it was apparent that more could be achieved with the expanded consciousness brought about by raising The Power of Sekhem. The Third Coda embodies that possibility. When The Power of Sekhem infuses every cell of our being, inner and outer, we access the Akashic Records and co-create a new world.

The Third Coda

Akashic Transformation

Consciousness constipation passes[18]

Heaven above, heaven below; stars above, stars below;
All that is above, thus also below; understand this and be blessed.
Kircher, *Prodrom Copt.*[19]

Constipated consciousness. A beautifully descriptive phrase. A perfect metaphor for being stuck in the lack-of-wider-awareness state that precedes the raising of the Power of Sekhem and expanding out into the multidimensions of consciousness. As I write, in late November 2017, Saturn, the Lord of Karma and Time, is passing across the galactic centre, the point around which our galaxy is rotating. It is joined by Mercury, the planet of the mind and mental conditioning. Mercury is hovering over the galactic centre, about to station before going retrograde (apparently moving backwards in the sky). Old patterns are reviewed, outdated beliefs erased, and new ones inputted. In esoteric astrology, Saturn is also the occult Ring-Pass-Not. A boundary that is transcended only through initiation, opening the way to bringing cosmic wisdom and all that lies beyond 'down to earth'. Once initiation is complete, we become conscious co-creators.

The galactic centre lies in the Milky Way, the 'road to the stars' of the ancient Egyptians. On the day the manuscript is uploaded to the publisher, from the astrological perspective, the sun, new moon and Venus will also be passing over this point. The sun is our soul intention, our inner light. The moon is our past, our emotional conditioning, when it's new something fresh emerges. Venus is unconditional love – amongst other things. Venus can also be uncontrolled lust and avaricious desire. She was a goddess with many facets to her nature.

This is a potent moment for consciously anchoring the raised vibrations of 'above' into the earth 'below' to upgrade our awareness and bring in a new paradigm. Fortunately the effects of the planetary activation will continue for some time yet, gradually winding down until the next Saturn-galactic-centre conjunction in twenty-eight years' time – yet reactivated each year as the sun passes the same point.

The galactic centre is known as 'the Sun of our sun', the point around which our solar system – and our soul consciousness – revolves. In other words, the sun at the centre of our solar system maintains the same relationship to the galactic centre as our earth does to the sun. The microcosm echoes the macrocosm, 'as within, so without' in the words of the ancient Egyptian sage Hermes Trismegistus. In ancient Egyptian terms, it is Amun-Ra who resides at the centre of all things. 'He' is the godhead, the 'Absolute', All That Is. The galactic centre has been described as "a conduit to the most creative force that exists in oneself and in our collective destiny... a super massive black hole, a galactic gravitational centre, a huge cosmic womb."[20] Many astrologers regard it as a transmitter of 'Divine Consciousness', an access point to transcendental awareness. So much is birthed here. It is a source of immense energy, motivation, and aspiration.

Saturn passing over this point reminds us that we are each individually responsible for healing the present, releasing the karma of the past, letting go of old emotional wounds and traumas to create a better future for all. In the process, metaphysical 'defragging' is required. A release not only of mental, emotional and physical traumas and ingrained toxic patterns from the past, but also the belief systems and faulty concepts that hold us tied to a three-dimensional view of the world. This transformation is quickly achieved by accessing and defragging the Akashic Records. *The Alchemy of Night* offers us a way to fulfil Saturn's demands by raising our awareness and co-creating a new universe – within and without.

Bringing heaven to earth

Once the Power of Sekhem is mastered, we discover that we do not have to go anywhere in order to experience the interconnectedness of all things, however. 'Absolute Oneness' is instantly available. As is the Akashic Record. It is within us, permeating every cell of our being – and the intercellular spaces in between that *are* higher consciousness. A new world has literally been opened to us. We are a manifestation of divine, sacred consciousness on earth. Everything is possible. This is an insight that crystals have been offering us since the world began. *Everything* in our universe – and beyond – is alive, sentient and conscious. This was sacred knowledge in the ancient world, but was rejected as outdated and unsophisticated as modern religions and the science of the 'Enlightenment' took over. Personally, I prefer the term 'Endarkenment'.[21] It sums up so precisely the lack of light and metaphysical insight that besets the modern world. This, however, can be transmuted and the arcane knowledge returned to awareness, bringing the sacred into the everyday. It infuses our planet with the transcendental Flame of Expanded Awareness.

The Akashic Record

The Akashic Record is the ongoing story of the soul, the ancestors, the planet and All That Is. Holographic, each tiny piece encompasses the whole. Our souls are connected to this hologram, each carrying a fragment that contains the whole. Reading it gives you an overview – or a microscopic thumbnail. The Record is not fixed. It is fluid and transmutable. Functioning rather like a cosmic computer program that runs in the background, it holds the memory of everything that ever has been, could be, or will be. All possibilities, probabilities and improbabilities are woven into its fabric. In ancient Egypt the Record was kept by the ibis-headed god Thoth (Tjehuti). Like a computer that badly needs an upgrade, the Record becomes clogged and outdated, littered with bits of programming that are no longer relevant. Defragging becomes necessary. Fortunately the Power of Sekhem does this for you.

The Inner Akashic Record

Following the 'as within, so without' precept, personal karmic traumas and dramas, contracts and intentions, together with transgenerational memories, are also held in the so-called 'junk DNA' and the very cells of our bodies.[22] They are reflected in the chakras and subtle energy fields. The karmic blueprint carries the impact of all our experiences from life to life *in whatever dimension that they may have occurred*. 'Junk DNA', the subtle blueprints and the Akashic Record are part of our inner landscape.

'Junk DNA' is what gets passed down through the ancestral line so it's where we tune in to a vast field of experience much wider than our own. As it is found in each cell of our bodies, it has important implications for who you are, on many levels. Healing and transforming these fields returns our energy to a state of perfection and carries forward the soul learning, while at the same time healing ancestral wounds and so assisting soul evolution. Re-encoding your 'junk DNA' brings out its inherent potential and allows your soul's highest purpose to manifest. However, before that is brought into being, one more chakra needs to open.

Crystals for the Akashic Record: Amphibole, Ancestralite, Blue Euclase, Brandenberg Amethyst, Cathedral Quartz, Celestial Quartz, Celestobarite, Chrysotile, Cradle of Life (Humankind), Dumortierite, Eilat Stone, Heulandite, K2, Lakelandite, Lemurian Aquitane Calcite, Serpentine in Obsidian, Sichuan Quartz, Tanzanite, Tibetan Black Spot Quartz, Trigonic Quartz.

Causal Vortex ('Galactic') Chakra

Location: Above and behind the head to one side or other (dowse for exact placement or use a crystal to ascertain the position, see below).

Acting rather like a universal and cosmic worldswide web, the Causal Vortex is a conduit that accesses the Akashic Record especially that of your own soul and your ancestral line. Accessing this chakra illuminates the things you have chosen to experience in a given physical life and the soul learning you put in place. It is also a repository for ancestral and karmic dis-eases and these are healed through flooding the Causal Vortex with the Power of Sekhem.

When this chakra is fully operational, it receives wisdom and guidance from spiritual mentors and higher dimensional beings so that the soul's plan for the present lifetime and any relevant contracts may be amended. There is no emotional involvement. Cause and effect is understood dispassionately when viewed from the perspective of this chakra. When activated and developed, it keeps the connection to your soul open and helps you access your karmic skills and abilities. The mind is clear and focused, allowing soul input, ideas and intuition to flow freely. This chakra brings the subtle and physical bodies into alignment and activates the potential carried in the 'junk DNA' and the consciousness between the cell walls. When the chakra is blocked or blown, you may be unconsciously propelled by your own past, ancestral or cultural imperatives or out-of-date soul contracts (see Appendix V).

Causal Vortex crystals: Ajoite, Anandalite, Ancestralite, Apatite, Azeztulite, Black or Blue Moonstone, Blue Kyanite, Brandenberg Amethyst, Celtic Quartz, Chrysotile, Cradle of Life (Humankind), Diaspore (Zultanite), Fluorapatite, Freedom Stone, Herderite, Lapis Blue Onyx (Scheelite in Calcite), Petalite, Phenacite, Prairie Tanzanite, Preseli Bluestone, Rainbow Moonstone, Tanzanite.

To open the Causal Vortex

- Ground yourself thoroughly and open your shamanic anchor (grounding root). Place a grounding stone such as Flint or Smoky Quartz at your feet.
- Ascertain exactly where your Causal Vortex is as its location varies from person to person. It may be way out in your subtle energy field or fairly close to the skull. It is usually behind and to one side of the midline chakras. Dowse, sweep around your head with your palm to sense its location, or use Blue Kyanite which 'sticks' or jumps when it reaches the chakra.
- Hold a Blue Kyanite or other activation crystal over the chakra access point. If dizziness and nausea result, breathe deeply pushing the energy down into the grounding root. This is actually an excellent sign that the chakra is opening and integrating. Placing an appropriate crystal such as Selenite, Flint or Preseli Bluestone on the soma chakra in the middle of your hairline may also assist. Wait until the chakra stabilises before removing the crystals.
- When the chakra has stabilised, use the Kyanite crystal to gently draw its end nearer to the skull if it was far out in your energy field. This chakra is more like a tube than a flat disc and can be extended down from the Akashic Record into a more easily accessible layer of the etheric body.
- When the chakra has stabilised, practise raising the Power of Sekhem up your spine to the top of your head and connecting it to the Causal Vortex. Three risings should be sufficient to integrate the chakra into your subtle and physical energy systems.

To close the Causal Vortex

Hold Flint, Hematite, Petrified Wood or Smoky Quartz over the access point to create 'shutters' over the site.

Bringing heaven to earth

- Put your shamanic anchor (grounding cord) and your cosmic anchor in place, linking them at the dantien just below your navel.
- Open all the chakras up to the Stellar Gateway and connect with the Gaia Gateway.
- Raise the Power of Sekhem up to your crown.
- Call on the god Thoth to be present to assist you and act as a guardian and guide.
- Open the Causal Vortex and connect it to the Power of Sekhem. You will then feel an electric, vivifying force flooding down to fill every cell and intercellular space in your physical and subtle bodies. This activates the Inner Akashic Record.
- This force heals, transmutes and rejigs the 'junk DNA' and the Akashic Record held within your cells and intercellular spaces. It releases ancestral source patterning, heals your own karmic wounds and those of the generations that have gone before and those that are yet to come. The transmuting energy flows to wherever it is needed. No effort or control on your part is required.
- Your consciousness is cleansed, purified and reprogrammed at every level, lifting your vibrations and the frequency of all your bodies, subtle and physical. Cosmic wisdom floods into your higher chakras and down to the earth. A new, sacred paradigm is established. The Alchemy of Night is complete.

Appendix I: Crystal Care

In accordance with Egyptian thought, crystals are animate beings and must be treated with respect. Paying due attention to the care of your crystals will repay you a hundredfold in terms of energy and efficiency. They quickly draw off toxic energies and, therefore, require cleansing before and after use.

Crystal Cleansing methods

Water
Robust, non-soluble crystals can be cleansed by running water. Place in the sun or moonlight to recharge.

Brown rice
Place crystal in brown rice overnight and recharge afterwards in sunlight. Do not reuse rice, compost or dispose of it.

Return to earth
Robust crystals may be buried. Mark the spot. After retrieving the crystal, leave it in sun or moonlight to recharge.

Sound
A singing bowl, tuning fork or tingshaws transmute negative vibrations. Sound over the crystal or place crystal in the bowl and strike the bowl. Recharge the crystal in sun or moonlight.

Smudge
Smoke from a smudge stick or incense cleanses a crystal before recharging.

Crystal
A large Quartz, Citrine or Chlorite Quartz, or Carnelian

cleanses and recharges a smaller crystal but will need cleansing afterwards. (Although Citrine and Kyanite are self-cleansing they nevertheless benefit from regular cleansing.) Placing a small crystal on a larger version of itself recharges a crystal, restoring its energetic frequency.

Light
Passing a crystal through light from a candle or visualising it surrounded by light purifies it. Placing the crystal in sun or moonlight recharges it.

Salt
Salt or salt water, unless in a salt ring or as Halite, is best avoided as it damages delicate crystals.

Purpose-made essence
Purpose-made crystal cleansing and recharging essences are available from www.petaltone.co.uk or www.crystalbalance.co.uk.

Alternatively, you could make your own cleansing essence by selecting crystals from the list below.

Crystal cleansing and recharging essence
Choose one or two from each list:

Clearing crystals: Black Tourmaline, Blue or Black Kyanite, Halite, Hematite, Shungite, Smoky Quartz.
Recharging crystals: Anandalite™, Carnelian, Citrine, Golden Healer, Orange Kyanite, Quartz, Red Jasper, Selenite.

To make the essence:

- Gather together appropriate, cleansed crystals, a clean glass bowl, spring water and a suitable bottle in which to keep the essence (coloured glass is preferable to clear or plastic). Use spring water rather than tap water that may have toxic chlorine, fluoride and aluminium added.

- Hold the crystals in your hands and ask them to cleanse you, your crystals or your space.
- Place sufficient spring water in a glass bowl to cover the crystals. Stand the bowl in sunlight for several hours. (If the bowl is left outside, cover with a glass lid or cling film.) You could also leave the bowl overnight in moonlight. (Note: although Selenite and Halite are soluble, place the crystal directly in water for this essence.)
- Remove the crystals and pour the essence into a glass bottle. Add a few drops of essential oil such as frankincense, sage or lavender and top up with vodka or white rum. This is mother essence. Label the bottle with the date and contents. Keep in a cool place.
- *To use:* Fill a small dropper or spray bottle with spring water. Add 7 drops of mother essence. If using a dropper bottle, place a drop or two of the essence on the crystal. Or, lightly mist yourself, your crystals or your space.

Activating your crystals

A crystal needs to be activated and programmed to begin working.

- Rub your hands briskly together to activate your palm chakras.
- Hold the crystal in your hands and wait a few moments to attune to it. Check out how you feel. A crystal in harmony with your energy field feels peaceful and calm, or buzzing and active. If a crystal feels unpleasant it may have triggered an emotional release, or may not be appropriate for the current purpose.
- Picture light surrounding the crystal and formulate your

intention. Be specific because focused intention is part of the alchemical process, but don't limit it. Add "this or something more for the highest good". Leave room for underlying factors to materialise. When you are totally in tune, say out loud:

> *I ask this crystal to cleanse, purify and activate whatever it comes into contact with. This or something greater for the highest good of all who come in contact with it.*

Maintaining your crystals

Treat your crystals gently. Keep coloured crystals out of direct sunlight, unless recharging, as they may fade. Layered or clustered stones could separate and points fracture or chip. Polished surfaces are easily scratched but tumbled and raw stones are more robust. When not in use, wrap your crystals in a silk or velvet scarf and put them away. This protects the crystal against absorbing negative emanations. It avoids a mishmash of crystal energies permeating your environment and allows space for those crystals that are working to function at optimum.

Appendix II: Attracting a twinflame

Calling a twinflame into your life is more satisfying and supportive of your spiritual evolution than seeking a soulmate. If possible, carry out the ritual in the relationship corner of your house or bedroom – the furthest right-hand corner from the door. Setting a time within which the rite will work keeps it focused in the now rather than eternally existing in future possibility.

Before beginning the rite, write down all the qualities you seek in a twinflame: phrase it positively in the present tense, avoid negative statements and wording such as 'will not...' When you are sure you have all the positive qualities, write them on to a piece of gold or pink card under the heading 'My twinflame'.

Requirements

For this rite you will need a twinflame crystal, which consists of two long, preferably equal, crystals side by side. The crystals may merge along their length, or spring from the same base. Crystals that have the same base anchor the relationship more firmly in the physical level of being, whereas two that are joined along their length but have no mutual base tend to attract a more mentally compatible, spiritually-based twinflame relationship that may not necessarily be physical.

You will also need four Rose Quartz candleholders and tea lights.

Preparations

Choosing a time when you will be undisturbed, carefully prepare a place for your rite. This should be somewhere you can leave the crystal in place when the rite is complete. Cleanse the space and the crystals thoroughly, including candleholders if these are crystal. Bathe and put on clean clothes. Place a clean cloth on a table and lay out the four Rose Quartz candleholders with tea lights lit within them in a square formation.

The twinflame ritual

- Hold your twinflame crystal and programme it with the intent that it attracts your twinflame into your life.
- Read your twinflame qualities out loud from the gold card.
- Place the card underneath the twinflame crystal in the centre of the candles.
- Then place your hand over your heart and invite your twinflame into your heart. Welcome the energy of your twinflame as it moves towards you.
- State that your twinflame manifests with appropriate timing.
- Then blow out the candles sending your unconditional love to your twinflame as you do so.
- Leave the crystal in place.

Alternative method:

Visualisation: Walking towards your twinflame

This visualisation draws your twinflame towards you, although it may take several moons for it to come to fruition, which is appropriate if you are working through *The Alchemy of Night* process at the same time. The preparation period before you commence is important. Do all that you can to prepare for this new energy entering your life. Be mindful of anything that emerges as an impediment or inner sabotaging voice. The quickest way to deal with this is Crystal EFT which taps out these old programmes and brings in a new way of thinking and feeling (see *Crystal Prescriptions volume 5*). It is important not to put a name or a face to the twinflame too soon as wishful thinking could so easily intervene.

Timing

Begin the visualisation at the start of a waxing moon – that is, with a new moon as the moon gets brighter and more visible each day. Practise it each day for a fortnight. Then at full moon stop for two weeks until the next new moon and begin again.

The walking towards visualisation

- Settle down where you will not be disturbed.
- Close your eyes. Relax and in your mind's eye take yourself to a favourite place in nature, somewhere with a long view – a path, beach or river down which your twinflame can travel.
- Spend a few moments enjoying the sights, smells and sounds of this lovely place.
- Then let your eyes move to the path. It is slightly misty.
- In the far distance, at the furthest end, you see a tiny dot. Your twinflame is approaching through the mist, which gets thinner as time goes by so that the silhouette becomes more and more visible.
- A feeling of anticipation and excitement seizes you; this is your twinflame approaching. Slowly, oh so slowly, the dot moves towards you, getting larger and larger as the mist clears. The wait is tantalising, your heart opens and you feel you can almost reach out to touch the figure.
- At first, the dot may be indistinct and not approach closely but in time the figure comes near to you. As it does so, the excitement mounts. You feel electric tingling in the air, a magnetic pull between your hearts and souls. So much so that you are drawn down the path towards your twinflame.
- In time, you see the outline clearly and then be clasped in his or her arms (try not to put a face to your twinflame at this stage). When this happens, ask that your twinflame

manifests physically in the world so that the two of you are together.

Remind yourself at idle moments during the day, or just before going to sleep, that you are walking towards your twinflame and that he or she is walking towards you.

Appendix III: Spiritual divorce

The *Alchemy of Night* process and the mystic marriage are intended to bond two souls together for a lifetime. In ancient times, the bond was for eternity. If you encounter a person with whom you made a mystic marriage in another life, it can be a powerful sexual attraction. A magnet drawing you inexorably together. But it may not be an appropriate union for the present lifetime and a spiritual divorce may be called for.

You meet someone and you're sure you were lovers in a past life. After two weeks with them, you realize why you haven't kept in touch for the last two thousand years.
Al Cleathan[23]

In a similar manner, if a present-life mystic or religious marriage has taken place, but the partners decide to part, a 'spiritual divorce' is called for. This process could also be followed if you suspect that a mystic marriage was made in a former lifetime, but you have not re-met that partner or that partner is not available to you. Simply use the power of your imagination to visualise 'the other' without putting a name or face to him or her. This practice is also effective if you made a marriage in a church in the present lifetime but have since parted.

Rite: The spiritual divorce

- When you are in a relaxed state (see page 22), picture yourself entering a temple or other sacred space. Allow the picture to come into your mind's eye rather than thinking about what it should be.
- Notice how you are dressed, are you a bride or widow? Either may be appropriate.

- Remind yourself that you are there to meet with a mystic marriage partner, previous soulmate, or former marriage partner, as appropriate. You have come before a priest or priestess to have the breaking of your union completed and blessed. If you are wearing a ring, take it off and return it to the priest or priestess.

- Looking at your partner, rescind any vows that you have made. Take back all those promises. If necessary, let the tears flow as you do so. Where healing and forgiveness are required, let these pass between you saying that you forgive unconditionally and ask forgiveness for all that has occurred without apportioning blame.

- If the marriage was one that involved joining the chakras, ask that the priest or priestess take up a sacred knife and cut all the ties between you, healing and sealing each place with divine light.

- If the marriage was a sacred, mystic one ask the Highest Selves to consent to the disjoining, separating and setting themselves free from the union. If there is any discussion, make the request three times, explaining that although the purpose may have been right and clear at the time the joining was made, it is no longer appropriate. Spiritual law states that such a demand, made three times, must be honoured. If necessary, ask the priest or priestess to take up a sword of light to separate the Highest Selves and assist the process.

- Say quite clearly, repeating three times: "I divorce you, I set you free. I become whole in myself." The priest or priestess will then bless your dis-union, allowing the divine energies to flow over you both bringing further healing and forgiveness.

- Say goodbye to your former soulmate, or ex-partner, thanking them for the part they have played in your soul evolution. Wish them well in their future. Accept their blessing and good wishes for your own. If appropriate, forgive yourself for any mistakes you may feel you have made. And forgive your ex.

- Feel yourself wrapped in the love of your divine, Highest Self.

- Turn and walk out of the temple. Accept the congratulations of those who await you. Be joyous in your separation. This is the moment when you reclaim your soul.

- When you are ready to close, surround yourself with a protective bubble of light. Feel whole and healed within that space. Then slowly return your awareness to the room and open your eyes. Feel your feet on the floor and your connection to the earth with a grounding cord going deep into the earth holding you firmly in incarnation. Get up and do something practical or have a hot drink to ground you.

Note: If you are dissolving a partnership that involves a written or a soul contract, amend the exercise to picture the contract being torn up and you both being set free (see Appendices IV and V).

If you are non-visual: Take off your wedding ring if you have one and find an appropriate way of disposing of it. Using a wedding photograph or drawing of the people concerned, cut the two figures apart, saying as you do so:

I divorce you, I set you free. I become whole again.

Allow forgiveness to flow both ways so that you forgive and are forgiven. Feel yourself wrapped in love.

Alternatively:

You could take a crystal heart that symbolises the union and split it into two halves (wrap it before hitting it so that splinters do not injure you). Then throw the pieces into the nearest water saying as you do so: "I forgive you and ask forgiveness for myself. Go in peace." Take a new heart and dedicate it to your own wholeness and healing.

Appendix IV: Tie cutting and partnership-contract dissolution

Tie cutting can be carried out with anyone regardless of whether they are still alive or active in your life, which makes it perfect for releasing people from other lives, as well as present life partners, ex-husbands or former lovers. Or, indeed, anyone who 'has their hooks into you'.

It is helpful to do this exercise with a current partner from time to time, even when you are in a happy relationship, as it keeps it clear and working well. Tie cutting does not cut off any unconditional love that there may be between the people concerned. But it does cut off all the oughts, shoulds, if-onlys, outdated soul contracts, karma and expectations carried forward from other lives, or the present one. The ties may be subtle and long lasting, occurring at higher vibrational levels at which they operate unseen and unrecognised.

The images you see are the subconscious mind's way of symbolically representing an emotional and psychic truth and should be accepted as such. Part of the work involves removing the ties, the place where they have been on each person being healed and sealed with light. The other part involves destroying these ties. The most useful way of doing this is to have a large fire, as the symbolism is important. As the fire burns, it transmutes the tie into energy which you use to re-energise yourself. It is also possible to use water to dissolve or wash away the ties. The one method I do not usually recommend is to bury them, as symbolically this does not free you from them, and they may well sprout and grow again. Having said that, I have learned from years of experience that it is impossible to be dogmatic as, just occasionally, a tie may be transformed through death and rebirth, of which the ritual of burying may be a part.

This work is powerful and should only be undertaken if you really feel it is right. It has been suggested that it may interfere with another person's autonomy and rights. However, the temple forecourt, in the visualisation, represents your own inner space. In doing this exercise, you are inviting another person to manifest in that inner space. They are there by your invitation, not by right – although they may well already occupy part of that space without your invitation, which interferes with your own autonomy. By using the circles you delineate the space which each of you occupy while doing the work. Do not let the circles overlap, or allow the other person to move into your circle. When the work is complete, you set them free and send them back to their own place. In other words, they move out of your inner space and into their own. Thus, you are each set free to inhabit your own space.

Crystals: You may find it helpful to hold a raw piece of Charoite, Flint, Jasper, Selenite, Green Aventurine or Obsidian as you do the cutting, gently sweeping it all around yourself. Anandalite or Brandenberg Amethyst held over your head when the cutting is complete fills your body with a new vibration. When using a crystal, be sure to cleanse it thoroughly afterwards.

Exercise: Tie-cutting visualisation

- Take time to relax and settle, breathing gently.
- Picture yourself in the forecourt of a temple on a nice, warm, sunny day. Really let yourself feel the ground beneath your feet, the cool earth below. There is a gentle breeze playing around your face, keeping you cool and comfortable.
- Spend a little time exploring the temple forecourt and then choose the spot where you want to do this work. You may find that a temple guardian makes him or herself known

to assist with the work.

- Draw a circle around yourself as you stand in the forecourt. The circle should be at arm's length and go right around you. You could use paint, chalk, light or whatever comes to mind. This circle delineates your space. (If you use a hoop of light, it can be pulled up around you if needed.)

- In front of you, close to but not touching your circle, draw another circle the same size.

- Picture the person with whom you wish to cut the ties and place them in the circle. (If you have difficulty in seeing the person clearly, picture a photograph being placed in the circle.) Do not let the circles overlap, peg them down if necessary.

- Explain why you are doing this exercise. Tell them that you are not cutting off any unconditional love there may be, but that you wish to be free from the old emotional conditioning, karma and bonds that built up in the past; any expectations in the present; and any no-longer-appropriate soul contracts that have been made.

- See how the ties symbolically manifest themselves – hooks, nets, tentacles and the like are common.

- Spend time removing them, first from yourself healing and sealing the places where they were with light, then removing them from the other person. Make sure you get all the ties, especially the ones around the back that you may overlook and those that are far out in your subtle etheric bodies. If you have difficulty in reaching, ask the temple guardian to assist you.

- Ask your Highest Self to check out the higher subtle levels as well as those closest to the physical and clear any ties that remain there.

- Pile the ties up outside the circle. If you have found it difficult to cut ties at higher vibrational levels, ask your Highest Self to deal with these on your behalf. Hand it over and patiently allow the process to complete.

- Now check to see whether there are soul or partnership contracts operating between you that are no longer appropriate or relevant. If so, ask that the contract either be dissolved or amended. (If this is a present life partner you are working with, it may be appropriate to negotiate a new contract.) If there is any reluctance on the part of the other person, ask three times and call in the temple guardian and your Highest Self to assist. Spiritual law says that asking three times will be answered. If you have negotiated a fresh contract, hand it to the temple guardian or your Highest Self for safe keeping.

- When you are sure you have cleared all the ties and relevant contracts, and sealed all the places where they have been, let unconditional love, forgiveness and acceptance flow between you and the other person.

- Send that other person back out of your space to where they belong. (If working with an appropriate present-life partner, they may well move to the far side of the temple forecourt to await the finalising of your process.)

- Gather up all the ties and contracts and find an appropriate way of destroying them. You may wish to have a large bonfire on to which you throw them, or a swiftly flowing river into which you cast them. Make sure you have destroyed all the ties and outdated contracts.

- If you are using a fire, move nearer to the flames and feel the transmuted energy warming, purifying, healing and energising you, filling all the empty spaces left by removing the ties. This is your own creative life force coming back to you in a released and purified form. Absorb as much of this energy as you need. If you feel able to, move into the fire and become like the phoenix, reborn from the flames.

- If you are using water, you might like to enter the water, or to use the heat of the sun to purify, heal and energise yourself. Then wrap a bubble of light around you to protect yourself.

- When you have completed the cutting, bring your attention back into the room and allow yourself plenty of time to readjust, breathing more deeply and bringing yourself into full awareness with your feet firmly on the ground and your grounding root in place. Have a hot drink to bring you fully back into your body and the present moment.

If you are non-visual: Place two photographs (or write the name of the person with whom you wish to cut the ties) within two circles that do not touch – you could use a large dinner plate for this. Place coloured thread or a net (the kind that fruit is wrapped in is ideal) or whatever your imagination tells you would be appropriate to link them. Carefully remove the threads from your picture and then from the other person. Burn them. Place a piece of Rose Quartz on each photograph and allow its healing energy to seal the places where the ties were. Then move the circles wide apart, certainly into another room and preferably out of your space entirely. If you were using a piece of paper with a name written on it, this can be burnt.

[Extracted from *The Soulmate Myth: A Dream Come True or Your Worst Nightmare?*]

Appendix V: Reframing past-their-sell-by-date vows and contracts

Old vows such as celibacy and other life declarations that 'I'll always love you' may need to be rescinded before love can flourish in the present. We may need to go back to previous lives and release vows that were made 'back then' but which still hold us in thrall. These include, but are not limited to, religious vows. Promises such as 'Next time we will have a relationship no matter what' or 'I'll never leave you' tie souls together for an eternity and may need releasing before a true twinflame relationship occurs and *The Alchemy of Night* is fulfilled.

If we desired something strongly enough, or if we fail to free ourselves from our vows, we could well find ourselves in similar relationships in the present life. The power of these vows is extraordinarily strong – and they don't always work out quite as the souls thought they would. The timing may be wrong, with a large age gap. The 'beloved' may be disinterested and reject all advances. The souls may never meet. It all depends on how well the issues were addressed in the interlife planning meeting – or, indeed, whether it was considered at all.

Perhaps the most pernicious of all the vows so far as *The Alchemy of Night* is concerned are previous vows of celibacy – and obedience. So often the libido became twisted and perverted out of its natural flow.

> *Although distinct from physical celibacy... psychic celibacy is a more pervasive and imposing phenomenon. It consists in keeping women mentally and emotionally at arm's length. Women can be exalted as wife, virgin, mother or deprecated (and enjoyed) as temptress, playmate, whore.*[24]

We do not necessarily have to go into another life to see instances of this, but the present-life experience is usually an echo of a former life. Religious vows present a huge challenge as many people have had past or present-life experiences in a monastery or convent. They vowed poverty, chastity and obedience – forever. Such vows were not rescinded on death. Then the former monk or nun wonders why, in the present life, they are always poor, have sexual difficulties, and feel powerless, at the mercy of someone else's control. When a soulmate comes along, they willingly surrender their life and then find that the lesson is to take control for themselves.

In male celibates especially, women were regarded as Lilith, the black temptress who sucked men dry in the night, to be avoided at all costs. Such repression can have a lasting effect. Or, women were put on pedestals as Madonna figures with whom sex was unthinkable. In nuns also, repression of natural desires could result in powerful sexual dreams, punishable by the church or exalted as 'visions' (see the writings of St Teresa for example). Carrying over such past life experience results in a background program running unheeded. Psychic celibacy may be practised, or denied and taken to the opposite extreme as overcompensation, despite the conscious mind and the soul's intention to enjoy full and appropriate sexual contact and the intimacy of *The Alchemy of Night* in the present life.

Renegotiating vows and soul contracts

It is perfectly possible to renegotiate vows and contracts from a present life or to rescind a past life vow, pact, or promise. The process also works well for soul contracts. Soul contracts are agreements you made with another soul in another life or in the between-life state. These contracts are not always beneficial in the present life; they may tie you to the past and could prevent you from being with someone with whom you have a more powerful soul connection and purpose, which could be for your – and their – higher good. As we all have free will, and as people and situations change once they are in incarnation and their personality and nurturing makes itself felt, it may well not be possible to fulfil a soul contract *but it may still hold you back*. Fortunately, it can be annulled or adjusted. It is not always necessary to consciously know what the vow was or to whom it was given. If appropriate, your subconscious mind will let you know during the renegotiation – if you allow it to.

Exercise: Renegotiating a vow or contract: the quick method

- When you are relaxed and ready, say firmly and clearly, out loud:

> *I hereby rescind all vows, promises, pacts, arrangements and soul contracts that I have made in this or any other life, or in the between-life state, that are no longer appropriate and no longer serve me. I forgive myself and set myself free. I also set free anyone from whom I have exhorted a vow, contract or promise anywhere in the past or who has willingly or unwillingly made such a vow, and ask their forgiveness.*

- Clap your hands together loudly to signify the end of those vows or contracts.
- Stamp your feet firmly on the ground, and walk forward freed from the past.

Renegotiating a vow: the more specific method

- Follow step one above.
- Picture yourself back at a point in time when you made a vow, a promise or a soul contract (if you are unsure of when this was, or with whom, ask to be shown).
- Rerun the scene as it happened but do not become involved

in it – see it as though on a screen. Observe but do not become part of it. Notice who is present and what you are saying. If it is someone you do not recognise, ask who that person is in your present life and what role they take, if they are part of this lifetime.

- Look carefully at that vow, promise or contract. Is it still appropriate? Is it something you want to continue? Does it need to be reworded, or rescinded? Is it something from a past life that has inadvertently been carried over into the present? Have you demanded a vow from someone else that is still holding them to you? If appropriate, ask for an advisor such as Thoth to come to discuss the matter with you. If it is a promise made to a soulmate or twinflame, have them be with you outside the scene to join in the discussion. Check whether it needs to continue. Check also whether you made a promise to, or a contract with, a soulmate or twinflame between lives.

- Then see yourself back in that scene using new wording. Be firm and clear: "*It is for this life only, for as long as appropriate.*" If a soul contract cannot continue, set out why it is no longer appropriate. Or state clearly: "I cannot do that" if what you are being asked will fetter your soul unreasonably.

- If the vow or contract has to carry over into the present life, or if it has been made for or in the present life, set out the conditions under which it operates, and state firmly that it will be released when no longer appropriate. If the contract is to continue, make it clear that if your soulmate, or the other person, does not stick to the new terms of agreement, or if circumstances change, then the vow or contract will no longer apply.

- When you are sure that the scene has been reframed and the vow or contract renegotiated to your satisfaction, let it go with forgiveness.

- Bring your attention back to the present moment. Take a deep breath and be aware of your body once again. Picture yourself surrounded by a bubble of light to protect you – use this bubble during the visualisation if you feel the need for energy containment or extra strength during the reframing.
- Then, when you are ready, open your eyes and get up and move around.

- **If you are non-visual:** State clearly that you are now released from all former vows, promises and pacts that you have made in this or any other life and specify those of which you are aware. If you are aware of a vow that you may wish to rescind, write it on a piece of paper and burn it affirming that it is dissolving as it burns.

Follow up this exercise with a positive affirmation. Tack up where you will see it frequently a note saying: *"I am free from the vows, contracts and promises of the past"* and read this regularly. If the promise was made to a soulmate, twinflame or someone with whom you are in relationship, discussing it allows change, and may bring hidden issues to the surface for exploration. Adding forgiveness to the exercises and affirmations strengthens their effect.

[Extracted from *The Soulmate Myth.*]

Further Reading

Books by Judy Hall

Fiction:
The Alchemy of Night
Torn Clouds

Non-fiction:
Crystal Prescriptions volume 4: The A-Z guide to chakra balancing crystals and kundalini activation stones (O-Books, Alresford 2015)

Crystal Prescriptions volume 5: Space clearing, Feng Shui and Psychic Protection. An A-Z guide (O-Books, Alresford 2016)

The Book of Why: Understanding your Soul's Journey (Flying Horse Books, Bournemouth 2010)

The Soulmate Myth: A Dream Come True or Your Worst Nightmare? (Flying Horse Books, Bournemouth 2010)

Judy Hall's Book of Psychic Development (Flying Horse Books, Bournemouth 2014)

Good Vibrations: Psychic Protection, Energy Enhancement, Space Clearing (Flying Horse Books, Bournemouth 2008)

Endnotes

1. See The Bremner-Rhind Papyrus: <http://www.british museum.org/research/collection_online/collection_object_ details.aspx?objectId=113956&partId=1>.

2. Taken from "The funerary papyrus of Henuttawy", British Museum papyrus collection.

3. The papyrus was painted sometime in the Ramesside Period (1292–1075 BCE). Papyrus Turin 55001 is known as the "Turin Erotic Papyrus" [<https://en.wikipedia.org/ wiki/Turin_Erotic_Papyrus>] because of its 'discovery' in the Egyptian Museum of Turin, Italy. The papyrus depicts twelve sexual positions that "fall somewhere between impressively acrobatic and unnervingly ambitious." See <http://www.openculture.com/2014/07/the-turin-erotic-papyrus-the-oldest-known-depiction-of-sex-circa-1150-b-c-e.html>.

4. No source is given for this assertion contained in a student blog on: <http://anthropology.msu.edu/anp455-fs14/2014/10/23/ancient-egyptian-sexuality/>. It is all over the Internet but the legend appears to have begun in 1992.

5. A higher form of psycho-spiritual consciousness.

6. "The Royal Ritual of Rebirth and Illumination: the regeneration of the divine king and the transformation of his Ba into an Akh", by Wim van den Dungen. See <http:// maat.sofiatopia.org/wenis.htm>.

7. Sir EA Wallis Budge, former Keeper of Antiquities at the British Museum. As the contribution by 'E.A.W.B.' was likewise dictated by Randolph, I cannot verify it – nor the banishing scene in which Sir EA Wallis Budge appears in the second novel. But I heard enough first-hand accounts of Budge's involvement in the esoteric practices of the late 19th/early 20th century from my mentor, Christine Hartley

(a Western Mystery Tradition high priestess), to suspect that there may be more than a grain of truth in it. A supposition supported by the Wikipedia statement, "Budge was also interested in the paranormal [<https://en.wikipedia.org/wiki/Paranormal>], and believed in spirits and hauntings." One of the hauntings of which Budge spoke made its way into my novel, along with Budge's great friend, the writer Sir H. Rider Haggard. Haggard – the major protagonist in the second volume in the trilogy.

8. Samuel Taylor Coleridge [<http://tvtropes.org/pmwiki/pmwiki.php/Creator/SamuelTaylorColeridge>], the poet and author, called drama "that willing suspension of disbelief for the moment, which constitutes poetic faith". The same concept can be applied to magical working and rituals.

9. Extracted from *The Soulmate Myth: A Dream Come True or Your Worst Nightmare?*

10. For further information on this cycle and how to utilise the rest phase to enhance your metaphysical abilities see *Judy Hall's Book of Psychic Development*.

11. See *The Soulmate Myth: A Dream Come True or Your Worst Nightmare?* (Flying Horse Books).

12. See *Good Vibrations* for appropriate tools.

13. Plato, *The Symposium* (London: Penguin, 1951) p. 6.

14. See *Crystal Prescriptions volume 4: The A-Z Guide to chakra balancing crystals and kundalini activation stones* for a list of the less beneficial effects of uncontrolled kundalini rise.

15. You can discover more about the chakras and raising kundalini in *Crystal Prescriptions volume 4: The A-Z Guide to chakra balancing crystals and kundalini activation stones*.

16. See *Crystal Prescriptions volume 4*.

17. See *Crystal Prescriptions volume 4* for further details.

18. See "The Galactic Center" on <http://www.philipsedgwick.com/>.

19. Kircher, *Prodrom Copt.*, pp. 193 and 275, taken from

online source article, "As Above, So Below", GRS Mead, Theosophical Publishing House, Adyar, Chennei (Madras) India. https://cdn.website-editor.net/e4d6563c5 0794969b714ab70457d9761/files/uploaded/AdyarPamphlet_ No106.pdf

20. <https://cosmicintelligenceagency.com/saturnatgalact iccentre/> and see <http://astronomy.swin.edu.au/cosmo s/C/Centre+Of+The+Milky+Way> and <http://www.philips edgwick.com/>.

21. A term used by Dr Patrick Curry during a lecture, "MA in Cultural Astrology and Astronomy", Bath Spa University in 2005.

22. See *Crystal Prescriptions volume 6*. 'Junk DNA' is the name that was given to the 98% of DNA that didn't 'code for proteins' and so was deemed useless. This is proving to be far from the case!

23. Source unknown but this quote is relevant to many people's experience of a spurious soulmate contact from another life.

24. Bianchi, Eugene, "Psychic celibacy and the quest for mutuality" in EC Bianchi and RR Ruether (eds.) *From Machismo to Mutuality* (New York: Paulist Press, 1975).

Take Me To Truth
Undoing the Ego
Nouk Sanchez, Tomas Vieira
The best-selling step-by-step book on shedding the Ego, using the
teachings of *A Course In Miracles*.
Paperback: 978-1-84694-050-7 ebook: 978-1-84694-654-7

The 7 Myths about Love...Actually!
The journey from your HEAD to the HEART of your SOUL
Mike George
Smashes all the myths about LOVE.
Paperback: 978-1-84694-288-4 ebook: 978-1-84694-682-0

The Holy Spirit's Interpretation of the New Testament
A course in Understanding and Acceptance
Regina Dawn Akers
Following on from the strength of *A Course In Miracles*, NTI
teaches us how to experience the love and oneness of God.
Paperback: 978-1-84694-085-9 ebook: 978-1-78099-083-5

The Message of A Course In Miracles
A translation of the text in plain language
Elizabeth A. Cronkhite
A translation of *A Course in Miracles* into plain, everyday
language for anyone seeking inner peace. The companion
volume, *Practicing A Course In Miracles*, offers practical lessons
and mentoring.
Paperback: 978-1-84694-319-5 ebook: 978-1-84694-642-4

Rising in Love
My Wild and Crazy Ride to Here and Now, with Amma, the
Hugging Saint
Ram Das Batchelder
Rising in Love conveys an author's extraordinary journey of
spiritual awakening with the Guru, Amma.
Paperback: 978-1-78279-687-9 ebook: 978-1-78279-686-2

Thinker's Guide to God
Peter Vardy
An introduction to key issues in the philosophy of religion.
Paperback: 978-1-90381-622-6

Your Simple Path
Find happiness in every step
Ian Tucker
A guide to helping us reconnect with what is really important in
our lives.
Paperback: 978-1-78279-349-6 ebook: 978-1-78279-348-9

365 Days of Wisdom
Daily Messages To Inspire You Through The Year
Dadi Janki
Daily messages which cool the mind, warm the heart and guide
you along your journey.
Paperback: 978-1-84694-863-3 ebook: 978-1-84694-864-0

Body of Wisdom
Women's Spiritual Power and How it Serves
Hilary Hart
Bringing together the dreams and experiences of women across
the world with today's most visionary spiritual teachers.
Paperback: 978-1-78099-696-7 ebook: 978-1-78099-695-0

Dying to Be Free
From Enforced Secrecy to Near Death to True Transformation
Hannah Robinson
After an unexpected accident and near-death experience, Hannah
Robinson found herself radically transforming her life, while a
remarkable new insight altered her relationship with her father, a
practising Catholic priest.
Paperback: 978-1-78535-254-6 ebook: 978-1-78535-255-3

The Ecology of the Soul
A Manual of Peace, Power and Personal Growth for Real People
in the Real World
Aidan Walker
Balance your own inner Ecology of the Soul to regain your
natural state of peace, power and wellbeing.
Paperback: 978-1-78279-850-7 ebook: 978-1-78279-849-1

Not I, Not other than I
The Life and Teachings of Russel Williams
Steve Taylor, Russel Williams
The miraculous life and inspiring teachings of one of the World's
greatest living Sages.
Paperback: 978-1-78279-729-6 ebook: 978-1-78279-728-9

On the Other Side of Love
A Woman's Unconventional Journey Towards Wisdom
Muriel Maufroy
When life has lost all meaning, what do you do?
Paperback: 978-1-78535-281-2 ebook: 978-1-78535-282-9

Practicing A Course In Miracles
A Translation of the Workbook in Plain Language and With
Mentoring Notes
Elizabeth A. Cronkhite
The practical second and third volumes of The Plain-Language
A Course In Miracles.
Paperback: 978-1-84694-403-1 ebook: 978-1-78099-072-9

Quantum Bliss
The Quantum Mechanics of Happiness, Abundance, and Health
George S. Mentz
Quantum Bliss is the breakthrough summary of success and
spirituality secrets that customers have been waiting for.
Paperback: 978-1-78535-203-4 ebook: 978-1-78535-204-1

The Upside Down Mountain
Mags MacKean
A must-read for anyone weary of chasing success and happiness
– one woman's inspirational journey swapping the uphill slog for
the downhill slope.
Paperback: 978-1-78535-171-6 ebook: 978-1-78535-172-3

Your Personal Tuning Fork
The Endocrine System
Deborah Bates
Discover your body's health secret, the endocrine system, and
'twang' your way to sustainable health!
Paperback: 978-1-84694-503-8 ebook: 978-1-78099-697-4

Readers of ebooks can buy or view any of these bestsellers by clicking on the live link in the title. Most titles are published in paperback and as an ebook. Paperbacks are available in traditional bookshops. Both print and ebook formats are available online.

Find more titles and sign up to our readers' newsletter at http://www.johnhuntpublishing.com/mind-body-spirit

Follow us on Facebook at https://www.facebook.com/OBooks/ and Twitter at https://twitter.com/obooks